WOMB TO GRAVE

A SHORT SPAN FOR HAPPY LIVING

DR. SUBHASHIS CHAKRABORTY

Made with ❤ on the Notion Press Platform
www.notionpress.com

Contents

DEDICATION

I dedicate this book to my father – Mr. DEBASHIS CHAKRABORTY, who now resides in the heavenly abode and would be a silent but proud reader of this book. He remains a role model for me for his commitment and sacrifices he has made throughout his life to enable me to grow the way I wanted to and is now the reason for what I am today. I cannot think of any better example of patience and persistence than my dad. He is the one who gave me the unconditional freedom to take decisions on my own. I also dedicate this book to a very special person in my life, My mother – Mrs. TRIPTI CHAKRABORTY. She is the one who has instilled the soul within me with infinite and selfless love. I feel myself the luckiest person on the earth to have her as my best coach I could ever think of. All throughout my life, she has nourished me with inspiration and encouragement to enable me, to face the world with strength and pride. It is the platform both together have provided me because of which I could celebrate and embrace life as I wished to.

I did not fully appreciate and acknowledge how difficult it is to be a parent until I became one myself. I am blessed to have two innocent and beautiful angels in my life, my daughters, SHRESHTHA, and PRATISHTHA. They are the ones who continuously motivate me to become a better parent and a human being which is a source of energy behind writing this book. I also feel proud to have a loving younger brother – TONY, and a new addition to my family, my sister-in-law – DEBKANYA whose presence and appreciation empowers me to continuously improve myself. My heartfelt love to my maternal uncles, Dr. Soumen Ku Moitra, Late Shri Ashok Ku Moitra and Mr. Aloke Ku Moitra who have walked the talk and have been appreciative to give me more power to grow. I am indebted to God for blessing me with such loving and unconditional relations in my life.

This book would not be complete if I do not mention the name of the pacemaker of my life, my soulmate – DALI. My life would have been incomplete without her. A deep sense of gratitude for her to stand strong beside me, as we learnt to survive and grow together. She has been the reflection of my confidence. Since we came along, it was she who has fuelled my drive. It is difficult to imagine even a day without her presence.

Finally, I dedicate this book to all my readers who have showered limitless love and trusted me to be able to contribute to their well-being.

I dedicate this book, **"Womb to Grave - A short span for happy living,"** to you all.

Preface

One fine day, a childhood friend called to congratulate me for the launch of my debut book – ***Happiness D'Coded***. She was from a disciplined and well-to-do family and had almost everything which a common man would have desired for. Academically, she was brilliant, passionate, and hardworking and had several laurels to her credit, both in her personal as well as professional career. In fact, I was honoured to have received her call. She appreciated the idea of selecting an evergreen subject of happiness. I had her agreement on almost every concept narrated in the book as she could relate each of them with one or the other event in her life. I also felt privileged for her trust in me when she shared few memories related to her personal life which she probably would have hesitated to disclose to others.

Although it was an interesting discussion, I suddenly realized the fact that she was fine with almost everything. This seemed impractical, at least with a person, whom I knew personally as someone very frank and transparent. After a while, I was sure that she was pretending to acclimatize to everything in life despite the hidden truth that she was longing for something. I got curious and wanted to understand her better. Wearing an author's hat, I took the liberty to question her, "*do you have any dreams to be accomplished in your life*?". I was a bit nervous with the pin drop silence for the next minute. It was a moment of self-doubt as I was wondering if I had asked her the right question or if my tone was appropriate. However, I remained confident and waited for her reply as I wanted her to think before responding. After a pause she replied with an assertive tone, *"Subhashis, you know, I don't want to accomplish anything, it's enough, I just want to be happy."* Her simple and short answer took me by surprise as I was expecting a narration of a long to-do-list of unaccomplished aspirations from an ambitious personality like her. The real conversion started and continued for long, and she shared her agonies and challenges without any inhibitions. But believe me, that single statement was a lifetime teaching for me! That day I realized that the most compromised element of life is happiness and accomplishments and achievements are short lived.

On one hand we hear spiritual gurus talk about detachment to attain the ultimate state of happiness and blissfulness and on the other hand we hear entrepreneurs talk about commitment to extreme level of passion and hard work to achieve unconditional success. Each one of them are correct at their place, but the agony is the implementation of these theories in absolute terms is difficult for a common man who is neither a guru nor an entrepreneur and would continue to remain a common man his entire life. There is no doubt that he has big dreams, high ambitions and craves for a peaceful and happy life. But practically he is entangled in so many responsibilities towards family, society, and job to make a living that he hardly has time and energy to spare for himself. He finds motivation in both the guru and the entrepreneur and is aware that a balance between happiness and success can result in a meaningful life. However, when it comes to execution, he has no clue how to strike that fine balance and there is hardly anyone talking about it together. He uses his own wisdom and experience to make genuine attempts but upon encountering life's challenges, he ends up compromising happiness in his hunt for success and finally ends up living a mechanical life. By the time he is enlightened with the wisdom to manage a balanced life, he is already exhausted and has hardly any energy or passion left to re-live his life.

Happiness is like a diamond which usually gets lost in a pile of garbage, wherein garbage represents the agonies and challenges in life. Every day we are in search of means to make a way to the diamond, but the garbage is so vast and entangling that we get lost in it. Interestingly, the diamond is slippery in nature, once found, it is lost in no time. Our search for happiness is nothing less than a rat and cat game which we keep playing our entire life in vain. Every individual is fighting in their own way based on their understanding and experience or based on suggestions and advice of others. We tend to find happiness in various forms such as money, family, job, entertainments, sports, hobbies, vacations, social engagements, etc. However, these materialistic elements are temporary in nature and fade away in some time. This results in anger, frustration, and demotivation as it requires a lot of strength, efforts, patience, and resilience to regain the same happy state of mind which is not easy. It creates a sense of self-doubt which challenges our understanding to find happiness. We are so engaged in our professional and social life that we forget to spend time with ourselves.

As a result, we turn out for instructions, suggestions, or

advice, thus creating a sense of dependence for almost everything happening in our life. We get influenced by the social media which depicts a cosmetic face of the society beyond life's reality. In this entire process we miss to establish a self-identity. We forget the fact that an individual's happiness is like a fingerprint which is unique in nature and cannot be replicated. The outside environment is too dynamic and different for each one of us. What works for someone may not work for me. Even thinking to replicate a similar ecosystem as other's is a futile attempt. The obvious question which arises at this juncture is, "does that mean there is no mechanism to find permanent happiness?". The answer is obviously a big NO! There is no permanent mechanism! However, the good news is: there are better, quicker, and sustainable ways as I have understood by observing and interacting with people of wisdom around the world. Unlike financial education, there is no structured education available to understand the ways to attain happiness. Moreover, due to limited time at our disposal we tend to struggle in our entire life. Therefore, this book is my sincere attempt to venture into this untrodden path to identify and structure some critical life management skills which could help one explore his or her path to happiness. In this book, I have tried to explain using simple layman's language, personal experiences, different stories, and practical tips devoid of any complexity.

I wish you all happy reading with "***Womb to Grave - A short span to live happily***" and wish you all the happiness in life!

Introduction

I am thankful to all my readers who showered love and appreciation for my debut book – *Happiness D'Coded*. Initially, I was nervous about my thoughts that I had poured in the book. But after receiving feedbacks, I was convinced about the fact that life's challenges are quite similar, and people are continuously in search of simple executable solution with a sole objective to remain happy. Sharing real time incidences of my own life, family and career helped me to connect with the common man and install a belief that not all challenges come to break you. The special elements of love, patience, perseverance, and the ability to look at life, not like sour cream but as a useful lesson/experience, has connected well with the readers. The book gave a hope to the possibility of balancing personal and professional life effectively. The book was also admired because it covered all relevant aspects of life together rather than the conventional process of sticking to one major idea or guideline. This further strengthened my belief that there is no maiden approach to manage life. With the feedback also came the wish list for the next book. On one hand it gave me the sense of fulfilment and on the other hand I could feel the pressure. The pressure was not exactly about writing another book but to keep it equally effective, simple, and grounded while working on a similar subject. One fine dawn when I was in the depth of my thoughts, I realized there is always a 360° view for everything and at a time you can only view half of it. That is when I decided to look out for the rest to research more on this ultimate objective of life - Happiness. This book gives you a different but simplified and practical view of the remaining 180° to complete the circle of *Happiness.*

There are numerous business authors on this planet, but I would like to draw your attention to one of the best and favourite of millions - Robert Kiyosaki. The mechanism which Robert Kiyosaki has adopted to impart business education to the world is quite unique. In his famous book – "Rich Dad Poor Dad," Robert Kiyosaki had discussed about a very interesting and impactful concept - **ESBI** (**E**mployee, **S**elf Employed, **B**ig Businessmen and **I**nvestor). While some are already aware of it, but for those who have heard it for the first time, here is a practical and interesting interpretation related to the life of a common man. As per the theory, world population earning legal money is divided into four quadrants, each representing the mindset of either an employee, self-employed, big businessmen or an investor. For the sake of easy understanding let us further simplify and club the four categories into two sets. The first set includes big business and investors who together lead the entrepreneurial world. They are the thought leaders and trend setters who influence and drive the economy and political agenda of a nation. They are always an integral part of national news, debate, and discussions of common man either for good or bad reasons. They are the job creators who influence the professional education system of a particular generation. Hope you realize how engineering courses in the field of IT were the talk of the town when Infosys and other similar companies started laying their foundation in India in the beginning of this century. Decisions and progress of such organizations decided the fate of the common man who typically work for them as employees or indirectly compliment their business or offer services through self-employment. These entrepreneurs are not only wealthy but also have ample time to spend the wealth as they have people working to take care of their business. Surprisingly, these people are just restricted to around 3-4% of the entire world population. To validate this number, check out how many people in your society own a luxury car!

The remaining 96-97% of the population belong to the salaried and self-employed category whom we generally categorize as "common man". This category is risk averse and try to contain their needs to their limited earnings. They believe or are made to believe in being educated to be able to take up a good job, earn well, support family, nurture the next generation and secure the future financially. Unlike the big businessmen and investors, these people are dependent on their own time and skill to generate income. The only way to boost their income is either to work more or attain higher skills. Therefore, they are engaged both physically and mentally all day either working extra hours or learning new skills. Therefore, they have limited or sometimes no time for relaxation, work-out, hobbies, family time, or vacation. They may have money but hardly have time to spend and enjoy the money. The situation worsens as one grows up the corporate ladder where the expectation is to be available 24X7 for the company. Other typical examples are people from the medical fraternity running their own clinics whom we consider among the accomplished class of citizens. Try talking to one such doctor to have a better understanding about his or her pain in personal life and I can guarantee you nothing less than a Pandora's box! Interestingly, this segment of the population find motivation in the success stories of the 3% population. Eminent personalities like Dhirubhai Ambani, Ratan Tata, Steve Jobs, Warren Buffet and many such entrepreneurs are idolized by millions of children and youngsters as they grow up to shape their career. Their life examples are included in the curriculum and highlighted by social media which further influence the young generation. As a result, they grow with lot of dreams and aspirations to become like them. Every person either wants or is expected to become great and successful by taking up extreme risk and challenges to achieve something different.

Interesting, while there are millions who give their unconditional best as if there is no second option in life, there are few who restrict their efforts to their thoughts. Unfortunately, the latter category is not covered in the scope of this book. However, the reality is that despite all efforts and motivations only few carve their way to the top. The percentage difference between those extremely successful and the others is extremely disproportionate and has not changed significantly since decades. There are multiple factors which collectively work to help a person climb the path to success. Let us accept the truth that not every person can take all decisions right every time, always stand up to his or her decision, have sufficient courage to pursue dreams independently, able to keep themselves unconditionally motivated, and can deal with people and finances with equal efficiency. We are all born differently and, therefore, exposed to different circumstances, environment, guidance, mentoring, opportunities, finance, and education. Big success has never been easy as it demands enormous sacrifice, and for most people it's tough to withstand such hardships in the journey due to multiple reasons co-existing in the ecosystem which is a vast subject of discussion. Statistics say that hardly 1% of start-ups are successful which validates the theory. Due to limited time at disposal along with multiple challenges, people tend to lose enthusiasm and acclimatize themselves to the routine life wherein the perspective of life suddenly condenses from "living for a purpose" to just "survival." They get so much engrossed into the responsibilities of the routine life that they let go off their dreams. It is also natural for a human being that at some point later in life, one would regret for the dreams which he or she could not pursue or achieve for whatsoever reason. Sometimes the regret is so intense that they start demotivating others. Although, it could be with a good intent, but they make others realize that there is no point in reinventing the wheel. At this juncture, a logical question that arises is: What if I am not successful in achieving my dreams? Will I be declared unsuccessful? How can life be still meaningful even after missing the goals that I had defined for myself? Is there any guidance available to lead a happy meaningful life that I deserve to live?

The state of mind is extensively diverse and enormously dynamic. It displays wide range of fluctuations at different stages of life, in different situations, and even at different times of the day and different seasons of the year in the life of same individuals. Thus, it is obvious that there cannot be any thumb rule which can unequivocally ensure unending happiness in the mind of people living in present materialistic world. In fact, happiness, like other mental states, is transitional. It is a lifetime challenge for every conscious person to retain and extend the duration of happiness to longest possible extent within the limited span of life. This issue is most commonly and popularly addressed by the spiritual practitioners and professional psychologists, interestingly who are also the victim of such fluctuations. Then what makes them an expert to be able to help others. The simple answer is they manage themselves well through continuous practice which helps them, not to eliminate, but minimize such frequent turmoil in life. Will it not be a great idea to at least start practicing managing ourselves for a better living?

This book is a sincere effort to help you navigate through a series of self-management approaches to sustain a happy mindset in this short span of life. It would guide you to reassemble your thoughts and draw a customized framework which would be best to deal with your unique challenges and ecosystem to stay productive. This book would serve as a practical guideline for all those who would like to revisit their life and give it a chance to make it more meaningful. Like my previous book, I have tried to keep the language simple and used live examples as lucid as possible to help readers connect easily.

Purpose Management

I

"The purpose of life is to contribute in some way to making things better."

- Robert F. Kennedy

A new house under construction requires a lot of experts like mason, carpenter, electrician, painter, plumber etc., to ensure that every part is built to its accuracy. What would be the fate of the house if every expert is working perfectly but independently? Although the walls may be strong and straight but may not be appropriately aligned for the carpenter to fit the door and windowpanes and for the electrician to lay the electric lines. Even the smallest mistake to the tune of an inch by anyone of them could result in disaster and heavy wastage of time, money, and energy to redo the entire structure. It's obvious that a proper planning is needed to ensure that such blunders do not occur. Therefore, before building the house, an architect is appointed to create the blueprint which defines the entire structure with all the minute details. I am sure that you have already started using this example in the context of this chapter to connect it to your life's purpose. You might be thinking that you need to be an "architect" of your life so that you can build your blueprint and work accordingly to ensure that all aspects of your life activities are synchronized in harmony. Sorry, but that is not the case!!! Please understand that even if the architect has prepared the blueprint, he is just another expert like the carpenter and electrician doing his piece of work. Once the blueprint is ready, he needs approval of the house owner to ensure that the blueprint is aligned with his expectations and visualization. Yes, now you are right!! The vision defines the "Purpose" of your life which you need to feel and own. It cannot be left to any external forces for its fulfilment.

Unfortunately, not everyone is blessed to have been born with adequate clarity of life. One day a traveller in a remote country town, convinced that he was on the wrong road, came to a halt in a village. He called one of the villagers and told him "Friend, I need help, I am lost". The villager looked at him for a moment and asked, "Do you know where you are?" he asked. "Yes" said the traveller. "I saw the name of your town as I entered". The next question posed by the villager: "Do you know where you want to go?" "Yes" the traveller replied. "Then, my friend, you are not lost. You just need directions". Many of us are in the same position as the traveller. We are clear that we want to build a house but do not have any idea about the design and, therefore, get stuck after a certain stage. Does it mean that the person is no more eligible to build a house? Absolutely no! The simple alternate option is to shift to Plan B. Rather than struggling with imagination, the person needs to visit ready flats created by experienced reality estate builders. The person needs to keenly observe the varieties available to either build his own house or purchase one which provides maximum satisfaction. That is how "Purpose" needs to be managed. You will have to spend sufficient time in listening to learned people and observing your surroundings. It would help you to discover and explore new ideas that syncs with your deeper senses and enable you to stay motivated unconditionally. A clear purpose prevents you from falling in life and even if you fall it has enough power to re-energize you to rise and get back on track.

I am one of those people who has used a Plan B. I still remember the moment during my university induction when the principal asked each student to introduce themselves. While everyone introduced their name, state of residence, and hobbies, I was very excited to make my introduction a little interesting. When it turned to me, I introduced myself by adding my innocent ambition that I would like to be the Vice President of a Pharma company. Although the principal did not appreciate publicly but his expression said it all! Interestingly, one of my good friends remembers the incidence even after 25 years. That single moment of self-declaration in public had a strong influence on me. As a novice, I carried this as my Purpose during the entire study tenure which kept me motivated to maintain a decent academic career with distinction. However, after getting into a job and working for few years I encountered the brutal realities of the corporate world and the so-called Purpose started diluting. Meanwhile, I had started reading self-help books and attended leadership sessions which gave me an access to the wisdoms of life. During this period, I also developed the interest to write and had published my first self-help book. My life took a different turn once people started giving me feedback of my book. They gained trust to share their life's ambitions, wishes, challenges, failures, and accomplishments with ease. I realized that I had started to contribute to people's wellbeing by navigating them towards living a balanced life. I could feel that with every discussion I was getting connected with something important which gave me a deep inner satisfaction. My interest in accomplishment and acknowledgement at work took a back seat and was no more as important as it used to be. Honestly speaking, I enjoyed more by appreciating others and motivating my co-workers even if they did not belong to my department. I started taking interest in listening to their stories and in this process, I made good and reliable friends which I still cherish. I was happier when people reached out to me to discuss their challenges with an intension to find some solutions. It took some time, but I realized that my "Purpose" was found. It was all about helping people to overcome their challenges, take career decisions, provide clarity of thoughts, improve their living, and bring a smile on their face. While I read the book "Leadership learnings from the Bhagwat Gita" by ACE Simpson, I realized that in the journey of finding my Purpose, I had automatically inculcated the rare quality of servant leadership (service beyond self) which significantly contributed to refine my personality and behaviour. However, I have not given up on my ambition to grow up the corporate ladder as and when opportunity knocks at my door but without being desperate about it. My sole reason to maintain my career growth trajectory now is to ensure financial stability for my family and secure the future of my daughters.

It is important to understand and consider a fundamental aspect before you arrive at your "Purpose."

Please note that one thing which is beyond anyone's control is our birth. No one has ever been able to dictate one's time and place of birth. So, the first and foremost thing is to accept, acknowledge, respect and be proud of our existence in whatever circumstances we are in today and whoever our parents are. It is important for each one of us to believe that there is a supreme power which has already defined a purpose for everyone. It is a master plan and it cannot be changed. Constant complaining about almost everything or questioning our existence and things happening with and around us is equal to questioning the supreme power. A person who does not understand the sensitivity of this fundamental truth will always face challenge in establishing oneself and will never be at harmony with the external world. Therefore, a person needs to be in love and respect for the ecosystem in which he or she lives in. That is the first step to create a sacred environment to help yourself find the purpose of your life.

Purpose is quite novel and should not be mistaken with routine activities. Purpose is beyond earning money or achieving a position. Earning money is just a means to survive and enable you achieve your purpose. A car is not built with an intension to fill fuel but filling fuel in the car enables it to reach to its destination. It depends on a person's intelligence to deep dive into one's own conscience to understand what exactly he or she wants or what is that one thing which would make him or her feel accomplished. At the same time, it is equally important to realize if an individual is ready to get started on the journey to fulfil the purpose. It takes courage and determination to fulfil one's purpose as no purpose can be accomplished without intense involvement. Sometimes it takes years, sometimes decades and sometimes the entire lifetime to accomplish the vision. Therefore, purpose cannot be restricted or bound by the shackles of time and age. Otherwise, it would just be an activity and never a purpose. Eminent personalities around the world have taken decades to realize their reason for existence. The reason for calling them eminent is because they fulfilled their purpose which was beyond self. It was after the age of forty that Mahatma Gandhi realized that serving for his country's freedom was more important than establishing his career as a lawyer. On the other hand, there are revolutionaries like Bhagat Singh, Khudiram Bose and many more who sacrificed themselves at a very early age to fulfil their purpose to achieve freedom. Our purpose may or may not be as novel as those of the freedom fighters, but they are examples sufficient to realize the essence of Purpose in life.

My understanding of purpose is not only special but also simple. Sometimes, people consider that securing oneself with a decent job as source of earning is a purpose of life. I personally think that although there is nothing wrong in such a thought, but it could be devaluating the essence of the term "Purpose." Depending on one's financial circumstances, the priorities in life could vary from earning money sufficient to ensure two times meals every day to buying the next luxury car or a sea facing villa. However, if you analyse minutely, these are related to competition, either with self or with others, and that has nothing to do with the well-being of people/society/mankind. A journalist was in search of a story for her magazine. While having lunch in an open restaurant she saw two houses in the neighbourhood. One was a big multi storied villa with a colourful garden and two luxury cars parked with well-dressed chauffeurs waiting. The other was a relative smaller and dilapidated house. The interesting thing the journalist noticed was many kids playing in the veranda of the small house. After making a successful attempt to interview the owner of the villa, she thought of meeting the children just out of curiosity. To her surprise, she discovered that these children were kids of prostitutes. As they could not get a decent living staying with their mothers, the owner of the house, an old lady, gave them shelter with access to basic education and food. Finally, the old lady's story was the only one published in the magazine which needs no justification. It's not about being "wealthy", it's about being "valuable" that makes a difference. Your purpose would not only let people know about you but also keep you alive long after you are gone!

During my early PhD days, I was quite confused and was struggling to finalize the area of research. One fine day when I expressed my concern with my supervisor, he gently patted my back and told me that once I finalize my research topic, more than 70% of my PhD work is done, rest is easy! I understand the depth of that statement today in context of finding, one's Purpose. Buddha said, "Your purpose in life is to find your purpose and give your whole heart and soul to it".

Take up one idea,

Make that one idea your life,

Think of it, dream of it, live on that idea,

Let the brain, nerve, muscle, every part of your body be full of that idea,

And just leave every other idea alone,

This is the way to success.

Swami Vivekananda

Thought Management

II

"Your mind is a garden, your thoughts are the seeds, you can grow flowers, or you can grow weeds."

— ***Anonymous***

Time management is defined as the process of planning and organizing your time between different activities. Effective time management is when the planning helps you end up working smarter, not harder, and you get maximum output in minimum time – despite tight timelines and high pressure. Having said this, I hope you will not disagree if I say that we spend more time thinking than working. So, rather than talking about smart working, why not focus our energy to understand more about smart thinking. Remember that the body is a slave of the mind. The mind dictates and the body follows. If you can utilize the power of thinking effectively, work will be done automatically. So, your time is utilized effectively if you think productively.

Thinking may be of two kinds, one of which we call in Hindi as "*Chinta*" and the other as "*Chintan.*" *Chinta* means concern or worry and *Chintan* represents deep thought, introspection, and self-reflection. *Chinta* is unproductive which keeps you busy without business. The child has gone out to play, and the mother is spending her time at home worrying about him. The exam results are supposed to be declared tomorrow and the student is spending his time today worrying about his fate. An employee has responded to an email and now he is worried about how his boss would react when he sees it. The cricket match between India and Pakistan has just started, and the audience is busy worrying about India's defeat. Imagine the amount of time lost by all these people which could have been utilised differently and productively. Utilization of time does not mean that you must keep yourself busy working physically. Even relaxation of the mind and body is equally essential. It is ok to do absolutely nothing but without any worry, like meditation which is required for mental wellbeing.

Chintan is productive thinking which defines the essence of life. It questions, analyses, and finds solutions. The intensity to think deep is what differentiates a normal person from a person with intellect. Let us explore the **"Enlightenment Model"** which will guide and navigate you deeper into the productive process of *Chintan*. This model may also be represented as TLSE quadrants where **"T"** represents Teach, **"L"** represents Learn, **"S"** represents Seek and **"E"** represents Explore. Let us try to understand what these quadrants have for each one of us.

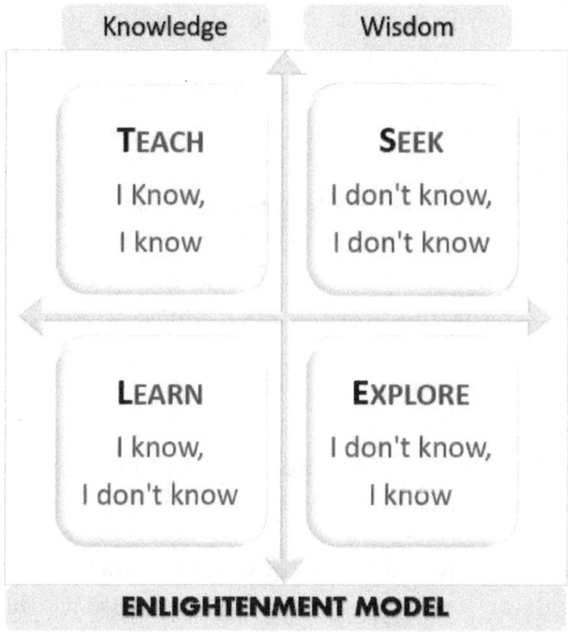

"T" Teach Quadrant – I know, I know: As responsible citizens, it is our duty to give back to the society. We should spare some time from our busy life to share whatever we have acquired by virtue of our education and experience, especially with students and youngsters. You never know which experience of yours ignites fire and makes a difference in someone's life. Supporting the development of even one person is worth a lifetime contribution. I recently met a young lady almost after three years. We got connected when she was trying to establish a business relationship as a supplier. The business deal did not happen, but we became friends. During our conversations, I learnt that she was struggling with her career and was desperately looking for a better life. Although I could not support her with a job, but I do remember spending some time over phone to share my struggles in life to give her some courage and directions to move ahead. When we recently met, she expressed her happiness with her new job and life in this new city. However, despite a comfortable life she expressed her desire to grow more and wanted to follow my principle of life, i.e., "satisfaction leads to the end of one's career." It was a pleasant surprise and a music to my ears! No wonder, I must have shared my thoughts during our earlier conversations which resonated well with her and got embedded in her subconscious mind. I smiled and felt accomplished that I could contribute positively to someone's life.

"L" Learn Quadrant – I know, I don't know: The world is changing fast. Our generation probably is the first generation who has seen the maximum changes within a lifetime. We are the living evidence to witness the extremely dynamic journey from postcards and telegrams to email and video calls. If we stick to traditional learnings and are reluctant to learn and adopt modern technology, then we all would soon be outdated. There are people who still have a phobia of using debit or credit cards and visit the bank for every single transaction which makes their life miserable. We need to spend sufficient time as and when possible, to upgrade our knowledge to stay connected to the continuously changing world, especially from a technology perspective. My father had never used any gadgets and had zero knowledge about it. However, just after his retirement, he called me to say that he bought a laptop and requested me to teach him to operate it. It was tough to explain everything over phone but respecting his enthusiasm, I took it as a challenge and started directing him to the best of my capacity. In the process, he learnt the use of MS word, emails, and basic functions of saving the documents appropriately. During phone calls with my mother, I often heard her saying that father is busy with his toy, obviously the laptop! It was after his demise that I came to know how efficiently he had used his newly acquired skill to meticulously document every detail of his savings and investments, that too secured with a password. He also ensured that the password is known to my mother. Post retirement, he used his time productively in learning new skill to adapt with the modern technology and used it for better documentation of his assets. Learning and upgrading skills have become more important than has ever been. A photographer may soon be out of business if he does not learn the editing techniques using different software. A surgeon would face severe challenges if he does not get acquainted to the use of hi-tech medical equipment. Our traditional Indian Post Office and National Banks experienced a major setback when private courier service and banking institutions started using the digital platform. Customers started shifting to these private organizations due to their superior services. It was recently that the government realized the necessity to train their employees with the new technology and stay competitive.

"S" Seek Quadrant – I don't know, I don't know: I believe in trying new things as they inspire, guide and challenge me to do something different which could possibly become an important part of my growth and development. One such interesting thing which I explored was entrepreneurship few years ago. It was a short journey but proved to be major turning point of my life as it helped to transform my personality to the person I am today. After getting started, I became a part of an elite group of successful entrepreneurs from different corners of the world who at some point of time also lived the life of an employee. I was soon nominated for a 3-day entrepreneurial workshop which was supposed to be conducted by the entrepreneurs themselves in a hotel in Bangalore. I was well acquainted with participating in seminars and workshops as it was an integral part of my corporate career and, therefore, I was looking forward to a similar set up as anyone would have imagined. However, upon reaching the venue I was overwhelmed to see a completely different and mesmerizing arrangement. I felt like I had entered a military camp with unconditional discipline, irrespective of your professional background. I saw that the entrepreneurs themselves were responsible for everything, right from cleaning the restrooms to conducting the workshop modules. They were on their toes to ensure that every participant is attended with equal love and care. Their humility was beyond imagination. Their energy was unmatchable irrespective of age or gender. They slept after us and were fully dressed to receive us at the venue in the morning. Every statement made during the sessions was hitting right to the heart and was helping me break my own barriers. Despite sleeping for hardly two hours a day, the energy of the trainers was so contagious that it motivated me to stay alert and absorb endless learnings throughout those three days. It was the first time I experienced the concept of servant leadership and realized its importance in the entrepreneurial journey. Since then, I became hungry for wisdom and got converted from a learner to a seeker. I started observing learnings in everything around me. At the end of the workshop, I felt like a transformed person booming with energy to conquer the world. The workshop helped me realize the worth of maturity, humility, energy, and wisdom, all woven together, in building an entrepreneurial mindset. I came to know about something which I did not know exists. The valuable time that I spent with myself in those three days is priceless and would remain with me till my last breath.

"E" Explore Quadrant – I don't know, I know: Recently, I was undergoing a coaching session sponsored by my company to support senior leadership positions. During one of the online sessions, my coach asked me "what do you mean by transformation?" She gave me an option to think just in case I was not completely prepared with a ready answer. I knew the meaning but still confirmed in Google. I came across few synonyms of the terms like change, makeover and shift and answered the same. Then she asked the next question, "When would you feel that you have transformed?" I did not have the option to search an answer to this question as Google knows the literary meaning of the term but does not know me. In absence of an answer, I felt nervous. So, I gathered some courage to admit that I don't know and was expecting an answer from her. With a very soft tone, she pushed me further to take some time to think. Now I started feeling embarrassed. Somehow, I collected myself with a heavy deep breath and tried to concentrate. Then abruptly I answered, "I would feel myself transformed when I am open to accept other's opinion and feedback with humility and find out possibilities to improve myself from what I am today." She immediately reacted with excitement and said "Bingo! You got it. You initially said that you did not know. However, with a little deep thinking you came out with the right answer. This means you thought you were ignorant but when you explored, you found the answer within yourself." Spending time with yourself for self-reflection either on your own or guided by a coach can sometimes lead to pleasant surprises and discoveries about yourself.

The Enlightenment Model represents the fact that to live a better life, we should spend time with ourselves and people around us. One hour meditation in the morning every day can amplify the productivity of the rest twenty-three hours of the day. A three-month upgradation course can accelerate the next twenty years of your career. Sparing half a day once in a month to teach students can contribute to quenching their hunger for knowledge and change their lives. Spending even ten minutes talking to an intellectual or successful person can leave an everlasting impact on your thought process. However, these people are difficult to approach unless you are closely related to them. On the other hand, if they are known to you personally, you would take them for granted resulting in no learning. Therefore, the best and inexpensive way to get an access to their minds and thoughts is through reading their books. There cannot be a better way to spend your spare time than reading self-help books.

A farmer cannot reap healthy harvest only by sowing seeds. He needs to nourish the crop with right fertilizers and water them all throughout its life. Similarly, if you wish you reap a better future, only working hard would not help. You also need to spend time to install a healthy and progressive mindset and take good care by allowing it to grow without any limitations. The journey of life is like driving in the dark. Although your destination may be clear but what you can practically see is a few meters ahead of you. The rest of the journey is covered based on your ability to drive and sustain the hardships of the journey which requires both knowledge and wisdom.

Information about the environment is knowledge but the learnings from nature is wisdom.

Relationship Management

III

"In human relations one should penetrate to the core of loneliness in each person and speak to that."

— Bertrand Russell

Let me narrate a short but meaningful incidence that I somewhere read related to the conversation between a young journalist interviewing an old teacher. As planned, the journalist asked the teacher the difference between "Contact" and “Connection". The old teacher smiled and apparently deviating from the question, asked the journalist if he was from the city. Upon confirmation, the teacher asked, "Who are there at home?” The journalist felt that the teacher was trying to avoid his question since this was a very personal and unwarranted question. Yet he said: Mother had expired. Father is there. Three brothers and one sister. All married. The teacher, with a smile on his face, asked again: Do you talk to your father? The journalist was quite annoyed now. The teacher continued: When did you talk to him last? The journalist suppressing his annoyance said: May be a month ago. The old teacher asked, do your brothers and sisters meet often? When did you meet last as a family gathering? At this point, the journalist's forehead was sweating. It seemed that the old teacher was interviewing the journalist. With a sigh, the journalist said: We met last at a festival two years ago. The old teacher: How many days did you all stay together? The journalist wiping the sweat on his brow said: Three days.... Old teacher continued: How much time did you spend with your father, sitting right beside him? Did you have breakfast, lunch, or dinner together? Did you ask how he was? Did you ask how his days are passing after your mother's death? Drops of tears started to flow from the eyes of the journalist. The old teacher held his hand and said: Don't be embarrassed, upset, or sad. I am sorry if I have hurt you unknowingly... but this is basically the answer to your question about "Contact and Connection". You have 'Contact' with your father, but you do not have 'Connection' with him. You are not connected to him. Connection is between hearts. It is about sitting together, sharing meals, caring for each other, touching, shaking hands, having eye contact, and spending some time together. All your brothers and sisters have 'Contact' but no 'Connection' with each other. The journalist wiped his eyes and said: Thanks Sir for teaching me a fine and unforgettable lesson. This is the reality today. Whether at home, office or in the society, everybody has lots of contacts but there is no connection. Everybody is busy in his or her own world. Let us not maintain just "Contacts" but let us remain "Connected." Caring, sharing, and spending time with all our dear ones is the need of the hour. Having said this, it is also important that we stay away from negative people as they have a problem for every solution.

Our mind is always curious and eager to gain information. If the information is used wisely and at the right time, it can help a person face challenge and survive effectively. However, there is always another side of the coin wherein if the same information is not managed well, could create troubles. The trouble starts when we are unable to differentiate between which information to pick and which not. To be specific, it is about that information which has nothing to do with an individual's growth or betterment of the society. People tend to indulge in processing unnecessary information when they are neither occupied in life nor have any intention to do something meaningful. This is when the mind, which is still operational, becomes interested in gathering information beyond a point of necessity about relatives, colleagues, ex-colleagues, peers, friends, enemies, neighbours, etc. Hope you understand the point which I am trying to make. I am quite sure that this is not a difficult subject to understand for anyone living on this planet, even with limited wisdom. A small incidence in my life will help you to understand the implication of information on relationships.

We recently celebrated our silver jubilee at the school which is in a very small town in the eastern part of India. It was a nostalgic and emotional experience to visit the place where we spend a large portion of our life. One of my dearest friends, a decent businessman in the same town, was very excited to meet me and he made sure that I am introduced to his family and office staff. I was very happy with the experience, and we were having a very good time. One evening, we went for site seeing when we got some time to talk to each other in peace. He was quite inquisitive to know about my journey from school to the corporate world. I was equally excited narrating the challenges I faced in the journey and how I overcame them. He was hearing with patience when suddenly he interrupted me and asked me about my pay cheque. Honestly speaking, I was shocked and was very embarrassed as this was the first time, I had encountered such an intimidating question. However, I collected myself and since I sensed innocence in his voice, I responded indirectly by sharing some indicators of corporate salary structures in metro cities. While I was trying to explain him, he seemed to have subconsciously processed the information to arrive to a certain salary structure. That is where the mood around the entire conversation changed. I am not sure about his calculation, but one thing was sure that he had already created a status gap between us. I could feel that his involvement in my story was already lost. Although we were there together for the next two days but we could never get along. It was then that I realized the intention for all those visits to his home and workplace. I am sure you can connect to many similar examples in your own life.

Often, conversation between two people revolves around a third person which we call gossip. You may not be aware, but such conversations get so deeply implanted in the subconscious mind that it gets played back at a time when you are supposed to be with yourself or wish to relax. Unfortunately, living in a social environment, it is quite difficult to avoid such kind of conversations, unless you are a monk or priest or socially detached. So, the solution left is to manage such situations effectively. I call the solution as the "Power of Ignorance." Let us not be unnecessarily bothered or involved in other's personal life or career unless the person approaches you for suggestion or support. It is important to suppress our inherent impulsive behaviour of gathering unnecessary information by strengthening the power of ignorance. I am sure a lot of tensions, based on the ground of superiority or inferiority complex, between relatives will get addressed by this. Differences between colleagues at work can be eased out resulting in a more friendly and cordial working environment. Overall, the acceptance and respect for others in our life would improve and would in turn help in developing a much more peaceful society. Sometimes less information is better for healthy and peaceful living!

The fundamental fact behind an ideal relationship is related to love and care for people around us. However, as always said, excess of anything is dangerous. Similarly, excess love and care in any relationship could prove detrimental. People with such intense feelings are said to be possessive. It could also be defined as a kind of attachment where there is hardly scope for detachment. Such feelings are usually observed in parents who are over-caring and overprotective in nature. The impact is negative for both the parent and the child. Due to excessive pampering, the child is shielded from facing the challenges and realities of life. Living under constant surveillance, the child never gets to express his or her opinion and implement his or her decisions. On the other hand, kids miss the chance to live their own life when their parents are over-concerned about their child's wellbeing and security. Such parents compromise on their own hobbies, ambitions and dreams and miss living a life of their own. On a positive note, such possessiveness is required when the child is completely dependent and cannot take a decision at all. It helps parents to remain focused during the upbringing of the child. However, when the child grows to be independent, such intense feelings of parents if continued, get in their way of living. It makes the child feel uncomfortable and at times it become frustrating. Unfortunately, the child may not dare to express his or her feelings because of love and respect for the parent or due to fear of being scolded. Sometimes excessive love automatically represents being sympathetic which a person with high self-esteem would have difficulty in accepting and tolerating. The situation further worsens when the kid grows and gets into a relationship or gets married. Despite the best effort, the possessive nature of the parent makes it difficult for the son or the daughter to stabilize the new relationship in his or her way. This could probably be a major reason for the universally famous in-laws' conflicts! People consume so much time and energy in resolving these petty issues that they lose focus on the bigger picture of life. The irony is that people are completely ignorant of their possessive behaviour, and its impact on existing and new relationships. To avoid such situations, parents must have regular, open, and peaceful discussions with their children. They need to help themselves gain confidence that their children have the capability to understand, take decisions and manage themselves independently. Sometimes external consultation helps people realize that they are part of a problem for their loved ones. It is good to see this issue being addressed by many schools at the preliminary level by appointing fulltime consultants and even teachers are trained to indirectly counsel parents.

Based on the above discussions some of you may perceive me as advocating a self-centred approach of living. No... I am not! The world is because of beautiful people, and life is all about living with them in harmony. What I am trying to sensitize is, despite being the most intelligent species on the planet, our complex mind needs to be managed well, otherwise it can screw up relationships. People who are aware of this fact have control on their thoughts and actions and are the ones loved and respected in the society. They listen to their fellow beings with patience. They pro-actively ask relevant questions with a pure intent to understand others and not to narrate their own success, agonies, and point of view. People feel safe and connected while talking to such people and are eager to share their secrets unconditionally. The kind of trust that is built during these conversations become the foundation of long-term relationships. Despite having no formal training, these people automatically turn out to be undeclared consultants of the world. In many instances, I have heard my friends thanking me for supporting them during their stressful situations. Although I have acknowledged their gratitude but honestly speaking, I find no value addition from my end which could have solved their problem. I tried to observe myself during the conversations to check what leads to their satisfaction. I realized that I hardly contribute except that I just listen with patience and respond with empathy. In this process, people get a scope to express and share their feelings of every dimension. Recently, I tried this methodology with my daughter when I found her reluctant to go to school. After a long conversation in peace, she revealed that she was finding it difficult to cope up with the increased syllabus in her new grade. She developed a fear that she may lose score and would be scolded by her teacher in front of her classmates. Finally, my wife and I were clear about the issues and so could work on her subjects to destress her and help her overcome the fear. She now knows that she has someone who would listen to her with patience and support to resolve her issues.

Unfortunately, there are hardly conversations where one is eager to hear the other. One just waits for the other to finish so that one can start his or hers. Sometimes people are so excited that they do not even bother to jump between the conversation to narrate their own story. Such discussions are good to remain engaged but unfortunately are completely transactional without any emotions involved. Try keeping a watch on your conversation with your friend next time and I am sure you would experience a practical demonstration yourself. On the other hand, if you really want to visualize meaningful interactions, then try watching the conversations between a child and a grandparent.

We have no idea about people's sufferings. We hardly have people around us with whom we could express ourselves. Each one is trying to hold back their vulnerabilities to demonstrate a social image of confidence and happiness. The old concept of heart-to-heart conversations have become rare and cosmetic. People have inhibitions talking openly even to their life-partners for the fear of being ignored, ridiculed, judged, or rejected. We grow in an environment where it is important to mask weakness and glorify success. That is the reason children have bottled up stress and the youth suffer from anxiety and depression. As one grows up, these emotions magnify further due to lack of social support and true friends. Unfortunately, in today's busy world people hardly have patience and time left to just sit beside someone and are allowed to vent their emotions in the form of tears. Such support is considered as a waste of time. This was not the scenario with our ancestors. In absence of any social communication apps and tools, they had ample time to talk to each other as they were aware of the fundamental fact that talking helps. They used to engage not only in face-to-face talking but also believed in the just-listen-to-me concept by holding each other's hand, allow the other to burst out tears while just sitting in absolute silence next to the person who is confident that he or she is not being judged or ignored. During my uncle's early demises, I have seen relatives strongly provoking my aunt to cry as she was frozen in shock. We all know that suppressing grudges, agonies and anger for a long time can result in psychological dysfunction to any extent and dimension. The question to ask today is do we realize the need of such small but meaningful acts of social engagements in our own life. If yes, then are we ready to dedicate some portion of our life to good unconditional listening and allow people talk without any fear. Let us take a pledge to start talking again and contribute to the transformation back to those golden days to lay foundation for a stronger and long-lasting relationships. Remember that your relationships reflect your values. Build and nourish them carefully!

There was a farmer who used to win the award for growing the best wheat in his county. One day his young son asked him about the secret of his success. He told him that his achievement was because of sharing his best seeds with his neighbours. The son was curious to know why his father shared his best wheat seed with the neighbours when they compete with him every year. "That's simple," the farmer replied. "As the wind blows, it carries the pollen from field to field. If my neighbours grew inferior wheat, cross-pollination would degrade everyone's wheat, including mine. If I wish to grow the best wheat, I must help my neighbours to grow the best wheat as well." This also applies to our lives. If you want to live a meaningful and happy life, help others find happiness by spreading love, kindness, respect and hope.

Career Management

IV

"It does not matter how slowly you go as long as you do not stop."

· ***Confucius***

As a kid, I loved loitering around my mother in the kitchen where she spent most of her time. While I was fascinated with her delicious recipes, I was curious about her cooking method as she always used low flame to cook even when there was an easy option to quickly finish cooking using high flame. I knew this as turning off the burner was always my job! One day, I decided to ask her the reason behind this. While cleaning the dishes, she casually explained that the food ingredients do not lose their original flavour in low flame and there is also a minimum risk of the food getting burnt. While answering, she was busy moving around the house with all the household chores and I kept jumping behind her for more explanation. She continued that while the food gets cooked, she gets some time to finish the other household work. Otherwise, she would have to focus only on the food for which she will get stuck in the kitchen. This explanation was more than sufficient to satisfy a kid's curiosity but the real value behind the explanation was understood when I grew up. Someone rightly said, "slowly is the fastest way to reach where you wish to be."

During our PhD, my wife and I went to Australia for poster presentation of our research work in a convention. After the presentation, our plan was to tour with a couple, our college friends, who already lived in Melbourne. We decided to visit Twelve Apostles which was 275 kms away from the city. As usual, I was excited and anxious to reach the spot as I had heard a lot about it. During the journey, I got upset with my friend as he was driving too slowly. I tried conveying him my frustration, but he ignored and kept enjoying the drive. Having no other option, I continued with the journey in silence. After some time, I asked my friend to switch off the air conditioning and lower the windowpanes. With this the cool breeze started hitting my face which made the experience quite pleasing. We stopped at several points for coffee that we carried and clicked lot of pictures. We were fortunate to spot a Koala on the road which was a rare sight. Finally, after around 4-5 hours of drive we reached the destination, and the long awaited Twelve Apostles were in front of me. To my surprise, the view was no more exciting to me and was ok for me to start the return journey. I was struggling to understand the reason and was constantly questioning myself about this indifference. After spending some time at the spot, I understood that the real excitement was not just the spot but also the journey to reach the spot. I realized how much I enjoyed watching and feeling the enchanting bluish-green ocean on one side and the continuous steep mountain slopes on the other side of the Great Ocean Road. The same experience also helped me to understand the secret behind the excitement of mountaineers. While narrating their experience, mountaineers spend most of time narrating their journey to the top compared to the moment when they were at the top. Being on the top is a matter of pride but the journey is more exciting as that is when they overcome the life-threatening challenges by displaying right balance of nerve and mind. The same applies to our career. We are so engrossed in the thought of being at the top that we miss enjoying and appreciating the process of climbing the corporate ladder or entrepreneurship journey. Our impatience does not allow us to accept the fact that it takes time to grow and, therefore, we remain frustrated all along the journey.

When Chinese bamboo seed is planted in the ground, not even a single sprout is seen in an entire year. Surprisingly, not even a sprout is seen for the next 5 years. But then suddenly, a tiny shoot springs from the ground and over the next 1.5 to 2 months, the plant grows as tall as 90 feet. It can grow as fast as 40 inches every day and the plant can literally be seen growing. The main question here is what was the plant doing during these 5 years? During its dormant stage, it was growing its roots to prepare itself for rapid and massive growth. Without the foundation of a strong and deep-rooted network, the plant will not be able to support its upper heavy structure. We can say that the plant grew 90 feet in 6 weeks, but in fact it grew 90 feet in 5 years & 2 months. Imagine what would have happened if the person who planted the seed did not water or nourish it for those 5 years as there was no visible growth. Moreover, the strength of the deep roots is a necessity to support the heavy weight of the tall plant. The same applies to our career growth as well. It is important to continue watering and nurturing yourself with patience. No one has ever become successful over-night. Success demands years of dedicated hard work to build yourself sufficiently without which it would be difficult to sustain the success. Everything takes time and the time required to be successful is always unique for every individual.

I was attending an HR session at the annual global business meet involving senior leadership of the company. During the Q&A session, the participants started expressing their concerns about the HR's initiatives for career growth of the employees. While HR was committed to respond appropriately but the questions continued with harsher tone indicating dissatisfaction among the audience. That is when the Business Head stood up to support the speaker and address the questions. The first thing he did was to accept the dissatisfaction of the employees and acknowledge the HR's efforts made so far. But what came after that turned to be one of my greatest realizations in my corporate career. He said that while every employee is eager for career enhancement, the organization is also hunting for hard core professionals with sense of ownership and accountability to support company's growth. He cautioned that people who are ambitious to climb up the ladder must also be ready to take up the responsibility unconditionally. They will have to forget their comfort of fixed working hours; cannot complain of not getting time for family and vacations; not get exhausted due to continuous travel and working frequently in different time zones; take big and sometimes uncomfortable decisions etc. So, if one is ambitious to grow, he or she must be ready to burn their ass or else be happy with whatever they have as the life at the top is very different! And if someone wishes to validate his statements, they should interact with the ones already serving at the top to check out their work life balance. Are you ready for it? If yes, you are welcome to the league. There was pin drop silence and the session ended automatically.

It is important to be serious but at the same time there needs to be certain degree of flexibility in handling our career. Generally, our education, training and experience influences our career. For example, a person with research background continues in R&D for entire life and lands up being the department head after gaining a certain level of experience. Finally, we are recognized as a subject matter expert or a super specialist. The same applies to people with sales or management background. Most of my peers who started their career with R&D around 15 years ago, are part of the leadership team in different companies and have undoubtedly contributed to the company's growth. Such experts are needed, and these people prove to be the foundation for the growth of an organization. Being personally connected, I had the liberty to talk to them transparently and got to know their version of the story. The external truth is they are really doing well as far as salary and designation are concerned. However, the inner reality is none of them are happy. It is not that they do not like or respect their job, but they find it monotonous doing the same thing daily, month on month and year on year. Their expertise has grown to such a level that there is hardly anything left which is new or something which they have not done in the past. Despite being motivated by the organization in every possible way, they are left with no enthusiasm in repeating the same stuff. This is a serious problem in a growing organization as this results in converting an accelerator into a brake. Their saturated mind tends to block new ideas and lack tolerance to failure resulting in an unhealthy working environment. These people are usually the ones who sow the seeds of office politics. Therefore, it is not only the organization's responsibility but also of an individual with a growth mindset to look out for opportunities in different domains at regular intervals either within the organization or elsewhere. Nowadays, many companies provide options for cross functional transfers. This is a good opportunity and employees should take advantage of such opportunities to learn and use their experience in the new environment. I have a research background without any formal management training, but I took advantage of the organization's culture to explore multiple roles viz. techno-commercial, business development, sales, and product management. Its due to this diversified experience, I understand the mindset of my colleagues from different department and customers which in turn helps me build quick, reliable, and sustainable relationships. Cross pollination of ideas and experience by dissolving boundaries is extremely important for the growth of an organization. It is now a necessity for researchers to think beyond science and understand the market. There is need of special category of people who do not necessarily need to be experts but should have decent knowledge and understanding of various functions of an organization to connect departments together and help the experts to function as one. Once you are occupied in learning new things, the mind automatically becomes unavailable for unproductive discussions or thoughts, keeping you happily engaged.

While choosing career options, students can opt for cross-functional courses which are quite interesting as the scope of learning is vast, diversified, and interesting. The best example which strikes my mind is medical tourism. Can you even imagine in your wildest dreams to connect medical and tourism together but that is a reality today? Unlike the past, people are crazy for their health and have no intension to compromise the quality of treatment. The best thing today is that they have money and are very health conscious. However, they are unfortunate to not have the required medical infrastructure in their countries to support advanced treatment. Therefore, they look up to advanced countries and India has become such a destination. You can find patients from our neighbouring countries and Africa waiting for treatment in big hospitals of metro cities in India. They need support from people who not only help them to manage their visa and reservations but also understand their medical conditions for appropriate advice and manage the requirements accordingly. You could figure out more such options in other fields as well.

The conclusion which I am trying to derive is we need not stick to the traditions. Look out for options which are less trodden. The world is big and there are many new things to explore, learn and thus lay the foundation for others to follow and make your life meaningful more than you have ever thought of. There is no harm in thinking about establishing yourself as a big fish in a pond rather than being lost as a small fish in a river.

Asset Management

V

"The best assets can't be seen or touched; they must be felt with the heart."

– Helen Keller

In financial terms, "asset" is related to money, property, and any material possessions valuable enough to meet debts, commitments, or legacies. However, people of wisdom say that the biggest "assets" are those human qualities which helps a person and the society build prosperity over time. Money, property, or any material possession are all perishable and mere presence of all these alone does not make anyone wealthy. A person can only be considered wealthy when he or she understands the value of the possession, uses it rationally, keeps it growing and can recreate it if lost, even if it does not belong to him or her. Imagine you meet an extremely wealthy person who owns a property almost in every corner of the world and has multiple sources of income. He uses his private jet to meet his friends and throw parties for them. He spends heavily at auctions buying items to decorate his house. You meet another person, equally rich but with a difference. He uses his private jet to save travel time during business trips to meet his employees. He ensures their wellbeing and smooth functioning of the business. He also spends heavily buying auction items to donate in NGOs. Given a choice, whom would you prefer to spend time with?

Wealth is constant but its value depends on the beholder. It is not about having wealth but about having the wisdom to become wealthy! Our Ex-President, Dr APJ Abdul Kalam left behind 2,500 books, a wristwatch, six shirts, four trousers, three suits, and a pair of shoes. He did not own any property and survived on the royalty that he received from his own books and his pension. Still, he is recognized as the wealthiest person for the values he carried and shared with the entire world unconditionally. Knowledge is the most valuable asset on this planet. Knowledge and wisdom are assets often used as a synonym with intellectual asset and have proved to be a magnet to attract other assets. An individual's fame earned on the basis of money is shallow and short lived while fame based on knowledge and wisdom creates legacy. Historically, we may know Akbar by virtue of being a descendent of the Mughal empire but the person who is remembered in admiration and respect is Birbal who by virtue of his knowledge and wisdom held the position of consultant in Akbar's kingdom.

Let us try to get some hard facts cleared about money. Can you imagine living your life on this planet without money? You need money to meet basic requirements like food, clothing and shelter for yourself and your family on a day-to-day basis. You cannot deny the fact that money has always been as essential as oxygen. Probably you could use these two words as synonym when it comes to survival in today's world. So, let us try to come out of theory propagated by some spiritual gurus that "what is in money?"! There could be exceptional cases where one denounces his or her family and society for mediation on the foothills of Himalayas, but such cases are beyond the scope of this book to discuss. I would prefer to cry in my own house rather than cry broke on the footpath! While the need of oxygen is fixed, the amount of money required may vary depending on an individual's requirement. So, what needs to be addressed at the foundation of asset management is learn how to manage situations beyond our basic requirements.

It is a dream of every individual on this planet to attain a life of abundance. The most common three dreams are, a house, a car, and an international vacation and all these cost lot of money. However, there are people who shy away from expressing their dream. This does not mean that they do not need and wish to have wealth. Given an easy option, they would be the first one to grab free money. The reason why people shy away from such dreams is because they live in a state of self-doubt about lack of having the required skill or aptitude to be able to make it big in life. The other reason could be they prefer their comfort zone and, therefore, not ready to take any additional efforts to create wealth. In this process their family also ends up living a compromised life. These are the people who prefer to stick to their traditional source of income irrespective of multiple opportunities around. Rather than increasing their source of income they prefer to the traditional system of saving for future. There is nothing wrong in saving and is necessary to prepare for the future adversities. However, in absence of any intention to increase or multiply the source of income, the savings happen at the cost of compromising the present. Managing assets is incomplete without wealth generation. Inhibitions and fear in mind can never help in wealth accumulation. People who are successful have in some way or the other taken bold decisions and a leap of faith beyond their fear and comfort zone. Usually, we tend to live a risk averse life to safeguard our earnings, but the truth is that taking calculated risks, directly or indirectly, acts as an auto-catalyst to boost our income. We do not need to take big steps in an endeavour to achieve something substantial. Even consistent baby steps can help achieve something different at its destined time. With consistent hard work and patience, results happen over time, not overnight. Overcoming fear is the only way to bridge the gap between low and high-income and, therefore, "fearlessness" is the asset to be managed well.

During the initial phase of my career, I decided to take a break from my job for higher studies. My R&D experience was quite helpful in navigating me through the PhD research work. Based on the industry trend I was clear that after completion of studies, I would join one of the top Indian Pharma R&D as a Principal Scientist. I kept all my network active, to avoid last minute tensions during job search. In addition, it was clear for me and my wife that we would settle in a non-metro city to live a peaceful life away from all kinds of hustles and traffic. Interestingly, during job search I landed up discussing a very lucrative techno commercial opportunity, that too in one of the busiest cities of the world - Mumbai. Honestly, at that point of time, the offer was quite lucrative and unique for a person like me with a research background.

I hardly had any idea of this role, and I was extremely scared of shifting from a peaceful city of traditions, Varanasi to an active commercial city, Mumbai. Moreover, strong suggestions from peers to stick to the traditional career of research added fuel to my fear. It was extremely tough for me and my wife to accept this change, but we knew that taking this risk could be a gamechanger for our future. We weighed the benefits and took a bold decision to accept the offer. By God's grace, the decision taken a decade ago paid off well financially and has given me tremendous exposure to the places, people, and culture across the world. These all helped me build my personality and explore a lot about myself. One bold decision helped me to become fearless and come out of my comfort zone. I experienced the joy of freedom which motivated me to take many more bold decisions across my career. Despite lacking a management degree, I made yet another bold move from technical to sales which paid off well for myself and has set an example for others to follow. I feel happy when my peers reach out to me for guidance on managing career diversity.

Till now we discussed about increasing income by overcoming fear and leaving the comfort zone. Now the next stage is about sustaining the wealth including investments, real estate properties, land, cars etc. Leaving aside few exceptions, it takes a lifetime to create wealth and, therefore, it deserves a royal treatment. I believe that the best time to think about your future is when your present is good. People tend to ignore this, and their expense keep increasing disproportionately to their income. The problem now is not with income but with expense as most of them are unproductive. Any expense on big brands, parties, dining at expensive restaurants, stay in five-star hotels, expensive gifts etc., are unproductive. I am not even considering money spent on so called "bad habits" which is extremely destructive to health and sometimes character! The situation worsens when people take support of personal loans to fulfil their immediate extravagant needs considering repaying from the money which is yet to come. After fulfilling the basic and standard requirements of food, cloth and shelter, the only rationale left for any further expense is either "feelgood" or "show off." People lack self-control and become vulnerable to the society. The risk is higher for people with inherited wealth who have limited exposure to hardships of life and, therefore, have less value for money. On the other hand, there are people who despite possessing wealth are wise to have control over their expenditures. They spend only after a handsome saving and avoid debts. They spend adequately to live a standard life and their expenditures are productive like education, decent living, healthy food, exercise, health treatment, skill development, mental peace, investments, support to society etc. They use the money to sow the seed of prosperity for tomorrow for themselves as well as for their next generation. As narrated by Google CEO Sundar Pichai, his father spent one year's salary to book Sundar's flight ticket to America for his studies which is quite a lot for an Indian middle-class family. I hope this example is sufficient to prove the fact that extravagant expenditure is fine only when it is for something productive. This requires a disciplined thinking and living. Therefore, "self-discipline" is the asset to be demonstrated and managed which also sets the right example for the children to become independent and capable enough to build their own future. Therefore, true asset management is all about creating a fine balance between being "fearless" to make money and being "self-disciplined" to save wisely and spend productively.

We should all be proud of our culture and tradition that we as Indians have inherited. The biggest strength of our culture is its diversity. It is a wonderful collection of numerous unique elements including music, dance, food, festivals, clothing, religion, languages, architecture, and varied forms of arts. Its richness and diversity are a result of its million years old history of going through a series of idea exchanges with the outside world. There is so much to learn and practice. For example, our culture of staying in joint family prepares us to be tolerant and adaptive right from our childhood days. The festivals spread across the year help us to keep our lives colourful and engaged with people around spreading happiness and joy and strengthen our community. These all automatically prepares us to become a better team player in our professional career which otherwise would require a formal training. It is good to see that the present education system is giving equal importance to extra-curricular activities like, dance, music, art, drama, etc., which are all part of our tradition. Getting trained in all such activities is also about inviting discipline and structured thinking which helps to build a self-dependent and confident personality. People have built their career and created a fortune based on traditional music, dance and drama and have successfully established themselves as eminent personalities across the globe.

The current generation has already started realizing the need of peace and satisfaction. They enjoy visiting a village, tasting the flavour of water from an earthen pot, eating traditionally made food, listening to music from a traditional instrument, getting treated with herbal oil and traditional medicines and many more. A trend of shifting from modernization toward traditional systems is already on its way. The traditional system of Yoga, organic food, herbal treatment, meditation, etc., are the first choice when it comes to healthy living. Those who have realized the importance of our tradition and its impact on the common man have been wise enough to establish business around it and create their own source of happy living. I leave it to you to ponder on all those opportunities for yourself. We should be indebted to our ancestors who have laid a ready career foundation for us through the platform of culture and traditions. Is it not our responsibility to preserve and nourish them as an indispensable asset with utmost love, care, and respect?

Expectation Management

VI

"When you have expectations, you are setting up yourself for disappointment".

Ryan Reynolds

A young lady was at the peak of her singing career. She became quite popular at a very young age and was at the verge of getting television shows but suddenly her parents found a good groom and got her married. Although, her in-laws never said, but it was obvious that they wanted her to focus on the household matters to ensure that their son, being the only earning member of the family, is living a comfortable life. Being brought up in a traditional and cultured family, respect for elders was her priority. So, she continued to serve her family unconditionally by ignoring her career. Her husband, although very open minded, never dared to speak anything related to her career due to fear of annoying his parents. The in-laws were busy with themselves and had hardly any interest in discussing about her career. They were proud and happy to see their son doing well and were enjoying their post-retirement life. The lady got so much engrossed in the household chores that her regular practice started getting ignored. Years passed and the lady eventually realized losing grip on her skill which resulted in frustration. This in turn lead to arguments between the couple almost every day. Without able to bear anymore, one day she vented out all her agonies in front of everyone. She narrated how bad she feels to give up her singing career which mattered to her the most. Her mother in-law listened patiently and reacted with concern by saying that she never realized that music was so important for her. If it was so important, she should have spoken about it and accordingly a decision to continue with her career would have been made.

In one of my job assignments, I was given the responsibility to create a market for a niche technology in India. The technology was unique and interesting, and I was excited to position the company as a thought leader in this specialized field. I decided to create a "Centre of Excellence" comprising of a pilot lab with basic infrastructure and equipment which could be used to organize customer workshops and later publish scientific articles. The plan was appreciated by my colleagues and the stakeholders which motivated me to move ahead. I informed the premium clients that there is something interesting coming soon and they even sounded excited about it. I finalized the lab space, negotiated with vendors, and placed orders for the equipment, and everything was set. I wanted to have a grand inauguration along with customers working at senior management level and so invited our Global Business Head in Europe to attend the event. Upon receiving the invitation, he expressed his eagerness to know more about the plan along with few senior leaders. I took it as a good opportunity to present my project and prepared the presentation with lot of enthusiasm. Finally, the day arrived, and my excitement was even higher than before. My fellow mates wished me luck for the presentation. I started the online presentation, and it kept going without interruption. I was almost half the way when he interrupted and asked me to stop everything immediately using a directive tone! I was shocked to believe my ears and I sounded confused. So, he repeated with an assertive tone "Stop everything now"! There was pin drop silence before he started speaking again. He explained that this kind of promotion will compromise with the confidentiality of the technology and eventually we would create competition. He was extremely annoyed with all the participants to have missed to understand this sensitivity and act wisely. The boss was logically correct but the bigger question for me personally was what would be the fate of all the investments and how would I manage with the preparations already done!! A big expectation gap was already created, and it was completely on me to clear the mess!

There must be several such incidences that you must have encountered in your life. In both the above examples, either personal or professional life, all dedication and selfless efforts were in vain resulting in frustration, anger, and depression! Question is how can we avoid such situations? The subject of human expectation is a very complex topic as it does not have any measurement criteria. Something good for you may be just ok for me and vice versa. The gap between our expectation is the fundamental reason for most problems. The bee lives less than 40 days, visits at least 1000 flowers and produces less than a teaspoon of honey. For us it is only a teaspoon of honey but for the bee it is the hard work of her whole life. Hope you have realized that these differences are bound to exist, so we need to manage them effectively to our convenience.

Let us try to understand the expectation management mechanism using dual circle model. One circle represents "self-expectation" which indicates the milestones, benchmark, and principles that you have created and set for yourself. They reflect "You as a person" and you would like to maintain this image for your family at the personal level and for your team at the professional level. You consider these as the bare minimum qualities required to live life with grace and dignity. It gives you satisfaction and fulfilment and you would never compromise on them in any circumstances. You would always ensure to give your best efforts to maintain those standards. People who set a very high bar for themselves are the ones who create a special space for themselves in the society.

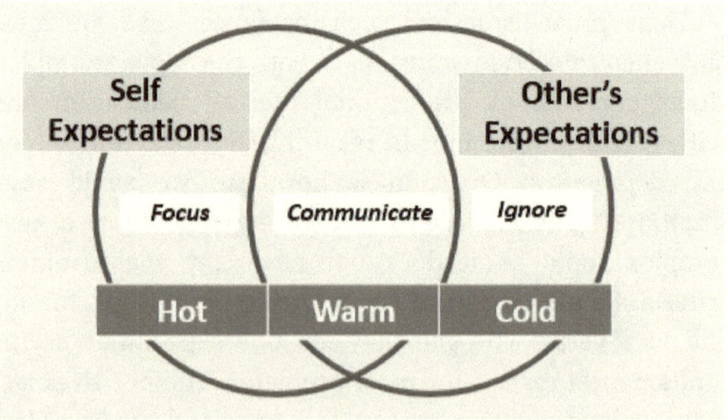

The other circle represents "other's expectations," which means what people expect from you. While self-expectation is an easy topic, people's expectation is equally difficult to understand for the simple reason that there are different types of people and we do not know what they expect. Therefore, to manage well, it is necessary to understand the depth of relationship with people around you. For easy understanding let us classify these people into three categories, "hot," "warm" and "cold." The hot category relates to people for whom you live and without them you consider your existence incomplete. These are the people with whom you share your good and bad times and discuss almost everything. Their presence directly influences or impacts your day-to-day activities. I am sure you would agree if I included parents, siblings, spouse, and children in this category.

Self-expectation automatically extends to the hot category because while setting your own expectations you have already considered them. If you have decided to wake up early in the morning and go for regular exercise, it is to make sure that you remain fit and available to serve your family. If you have decided to avoid junk food at home, it is to ensure that the entire family stays out of disease. If you aim to clear a tough exam, it is to make your family proud. In case of couples, one adopts the expectation of the other and owns it. If your spouse expects a home, you make all efforts with heart and soul to make it happen. When you expect your child to perform well in school, you make all necessary efforts to the best of your capacity to support the child. In these cases, there is lot of flexibility to willingly recalibrate expectations due to love, care, and respect for each other. Being engaged in these activities is a joy and watching each milestone getting achieved gives satisfaction and happiness in life. In case you find a gap in expectations then it is an indication to rework on your relationships to consider these people under the "hot" category.

The warm category is about people with whom you are in the process of establishing personal relationships and those with whom you are related by virtue of a relation or profession. From a personal standpoint, it could be your boyfriend, girlfriend, fiancée, in-laws, relatives and friends. Professional connections may be your boss, your team, business partners and stakeholders. When their expectations from you and your expectations from them overlap, it results in peace at home and office. But the question is how they would know about each other's expectations. The simple answer is "effective communication." Expectations should be truthfully disclosed, clarified, and documented in case of professional matters with an intention to arrive at a mutual space of alignment on the possibilities to fulfil them and setting up the viable standards. Without communicating expectations explicitly, one will frequently underperform in people's perceptions and even with the best outcome a "six-nine" situation would prevail.

The last, “cold” category is about all those beyond the “hot” and “warm” category like friends, colleagues, peers, relatives, neighbours etc. Can you imagine the vastness and complexity involved in managing the expectations of so many people? Do you think it is possible to manage so many people around you? Will it be possible for you to tune your behaviour and lead your life as per each of their expectations? So, in this case, the best way is to “Ignore,” not because you disrespect them but because you are not a superhuman being. However, in such case the high standard that you set for yourself would help you navigate and lead a life of harmony with the ecosystem.

Have you ever pondered about the major impact that the pandemic left behind? It has recalibrated the expectations of every individual on this planet. Many myths have busted, and realities have been exposed. One of the greatest myths busted is the expectation to be in office for efficient working. It is evident that if we leverage on the growing and advanced technology, we can manage work with equal efficiency and sometimes more efficiently from home, that too with flexibility and ease. Majority of the companies have realized this fact and adopted to the work from home concept. The concept of office is now considered redundant for many professions. Many companies have given off their office infrastructure and decided to encourage remote working. Companies have saved tremendously on travel, fuel perks and utility cost which has indirectly helped to reduce the carbon footprint on this planet. Talent hunt has become lot more easier and so is talent retention.

With such transformed expectations, you would realize how stupid many of us have been to travel to office everyday despite all troubles of traffic, health etc. Most of us have kept our spouse busy to ensure lunch boxes are ready before leaving for office. Imagine the extent of compromise we have made with our near and dear ones by not being available for them when needed. We have seen our children growing horizontally as we were gone before they woke up and were asleep when we were back. Weekends were busy just resting to regain energy for the next week travel! We have compromised our discipline in sleep and food due to frequent travelling. Many of us have missed celebrating birthdays and anniversaries of our near and dear ones. Unfortunately, many of us have missed to be beside our family members when they were taking their last breath. The good news is now the expectations have been corrected and many of us are able to avoid these unnecessary hardships of life and build a better living environment. In absence of pandemic, most companies have adopted to hybrid culture to re-establish the element of human connect and relationship. Companies which have reverted to complete work form office are sadly the victims of leadership who lack trust on their employees or are obsessed to see people work around them.

Sometimes back I heard a story of a poor old man who used to live on the footpath and manage his living by begging. His earning was just sufficient to keep him alive. One cold winter evening, a rich man while returning from work happened to see the old man wrapped in a torn dirty blanket. The rich man was kind enough to give him a few cents and promised him that he would bring some warm clothes the next day. The man went home and forgot. After a couple of day while returning home, he realized that the beggar was missing and recalled his promise made to him. Out of curiosity, he thought of enquiring another beggar a few furlongs away. The other beggar informed that the old man recently died. He also said that it seemed that he was desperately waiting for something and finally died shivering. The old man withstood several winters but missed this one because his mental strength to withstand the cold was broken down by his expectation for comfort created by the rich man. The moral of the story is do not commit if you cannot fulfil your commitment, as in this process, you never know you may be playing with someone's innocent expectations.

The past is an experience, the present is an experiment, and the future is the expectation. Use your experience in your experiment to achieve your expectation.

Success Management

VII

"Success is not a destination; it is a journey".

Zig Ziglar

On the 1st day of my 11th grade, my father and I were waiting in the hostel's common room along with my batchmates and their patents for the warden to address us. Due to good academic performance, I was fortunate to secure admission in BJB college, Bhubaneshwar, considered as the best university in the state of Odisha. My batchmates were also top rankers of their respective schools. It was indeed a proud moment for both of us to be a part of that gathering. We were anxious to hear the warden who was a well-known chemistry professor and an idol for many students. Late in the evening, the professor arrived with a big smile on his face. He greeted us with humility and requested us to take our seats. He narrated the history of the University and explained about the success of the alumni. Honestly, as it has been decades, I hardly remember the details. However, I cannot forget something very special which helped me lay the foundation of a growth mindset. He appreciated and congratulated us for being the high scorer or rank holders. However, these accomplishments are now a matter of the past and faster we forget the better it is. The present reality is we all have come to a stage where everyone is equal. It is time to prepare ourselves for the next milestone by committing ourselves to the same passion and hard work which has helped us to reach here. And if we want to be successful in life, this cycle must be repeated, after hitting each milestone. This wisdom is embedded in my subconscious mind and is fresh even today. He clearly meant that the top of any mountain is the bottom of another. There is no point of sitting on top of the mountain and bask under the glory of achievement as this excitement is short-lived. People who get stuck for a longer period lose their potential and ability to climb further. I found this wisdom so impactful that I promised myself to propagate the same learning as and when possible. Success is no more an event; it is a never-ending process that keeps life going meaningfully. Once you are satisfied, your life stops there!

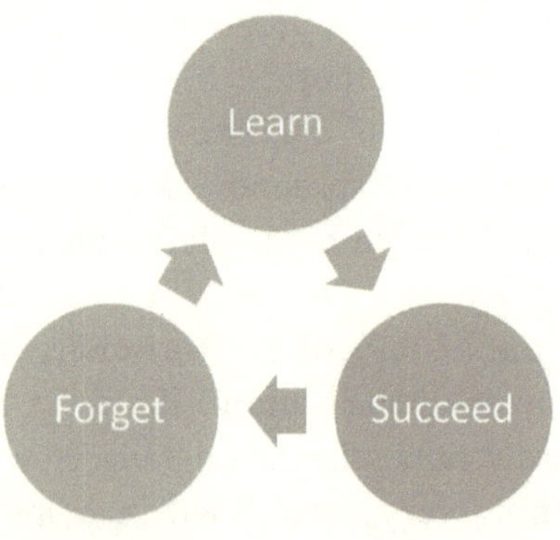

One of my colleagues and a good friend of mine was being considered for an internal shift to a key position even before the vacancy was declared. I was not aware of this development. When the vacancy was notified by HR, I immediately applied for it. Within a few days, the news of my candidature was an open secret! Due to my experience, I was being perceived as the top contenders. While I was waiting for the formal round of interviews, my office mates informed me about the frustration of the other colleague. One fine day, we happened to bump on each other for a casual talk. That is when he expressed his disappointment as the position was promised to him and now, he is being asked to contest an interview. He felt insulted and was even ready to withdraw his application. Honestly, I could do nothing to console him and somehow ended the conversation by saying that let us leave everything to destiny. The interview happened and I was selected. A year later I further moved up the ladder and he was offered the same position as my successor. I left the organization for further growth, and he also climbed up to a senior leadership position within the same organization. The reason for sharing this incidence is to help realize that success takes its own time! We should neither be frustrated nor miss the opportunity to fight to grow. However, our sincere fight should be devoid of expectations, and we should leave the outcome to destiny. Our fight should be strong enough to avoid a situation in life where we repent for not giving our best. It is not the success but the fight behind the success that creates the story for others to follow.

The pandemic took a huge toll on jobs resulting in a global crisis. Among these tough times, there were some people who did not hesitate to change their profession or makeshift their business to avoid a halt in their progress. They identified and explored new ways of life. They realized the essential needs of the community and found out opportunities to serve others and make their living. People left their comfort zone and started selling essential commodities. I have seen people from well to do families coming together to open online vegetable and grocery stores. One of my friends was quick enough to shut down his running restaurant business to set up a small mask manufacturing unit as masks were in demand and selling at high margins. He not only continued making money for himself but also engaged his entire restaurant staff to help them continue earning their salaries. These examples helped me to realize that we need to have sufficient flexibility to keep the career in motion which is nothing less than success under such extreme circumstances. All said and done, this is possible only when backed with a strong will and unconditional self-belief. If you cannot do great things, try doing small things in a great way as every step counts to keep you prepared for uncertainties. The world is evolving at an unprecedented pace and the only way to remain ahead of the curve is to remain a student throughout the life which would help prepare ourselves to new possibilities. Always keep a Plan B ready or prepare yourself for it. You never know when you need it. In addition, never even shy away from converting Plan B to your Plan A whenever you feel appropriate.

Success is a choice. If you decide, you would surely be successful at some point of your life. My grandmother used to say, "Aim for the moon, even if you miss, you'll land among the stars." Therefore, it is important to embark on the journey and keep going. But the issue is while we are quite enthusiastic at the start, we tend to fall back with challenges and failures. That is when we need self-motivation or motivation from our near and dear ones. Unfortunately, motivation is scarcely available in today's world as everyone is busy sorting out their own challenges. Therefore, if you wish to keep your journey alive, independent of motivation, then the solution is to embrace "discipline." For example, you don't need motivation to brush your teeth in the morning. When you keep doing the same thing every day, it becomes a habit which is the inception of success. The addiction of marathon runners to run every day is the reason behind their good health and fit body across their life. What you get by achieving your goals is not as important as what you become by staying disciplined in the journey. People get inspired to see how you deal with your imperfections by adopting discipline in your life. However, things that you need to keep secret in the journey towards success are: 1. Your big plan, 2. Your love life, 3. Your income, 4. Your next move 5. Your family issues. Never forget!

Let's try to figure out few limitations which could be a roadblock in your journey to success. Money is an outcome of two things: 1. Time and, 2. Skill. The amount of time available and skill acquired by an individual may be good for a living but not sufficient to achieve anything bigger than that. Therefore, if we wish to increase both, we will have to leverage on "other's time" and "other's skills." The simple point which I am trying to drive is never shy away from asking for help from the experts.

On the other hand, never ignore if someone is eager to lend a hand. Do not turn down the offer for a cart when you are carrying the load on your head. Accept help with humility. In a collaborative environment, your success curve shoots higher than your imagination. I respect the concept of empowerment in the corporate world as it allows to create the optimum space to leverage each other's expertise resulting in a high-performance team. You should also leverage guidance and knowledge of your superiors and elders to help you become successful. Thus, smart thinking can complement your hard work.

There is nothing called as quick money. In fact, "quick" and "money" are oxymorons, i.e., money can never be quick. Otherwise, everyone would have been a millionaire. There are no shortcuts to success and if it exists it does not last. It is important to stay focussed on one's expertise, build on diverse capabilities wherever possible and stay connected with the changing world to figure out new opportunities. These all help to generate wealth which is long lasting and helps to create self-identity and sets an example for those who are ambitious to grow.

Air Commodore Anurag was a jet pilot. During a combat mission, his fighter plane was destroyed by a missile. Fortunately, he was successful to eject himself and land safely with his parachute. For this incidence, he won many awards and appreciations for his bravery. Almost after five years, one day he and his wife were dining in a restaurant. Suddenly, a man from another table came and said "You're Captain Anurag! You flew jet fighters. You were shot down!" Anurag asked with full curiosity, "How in the world did you know that?". The man smiled and replied, "I packed your parachute,". Anurag was in total surprise and gratitude and started thinking if that day the parachute hadn't worked, I wouldn't be here today. Anurag had a sleepless night, thinking about that man. He realized that although he might have seen this person several times, but he never cared once to interact with him as he was a fighter pilot, and the other person was just a safety worker. So, my dear friends, who is packing your parachute? Whether we know or not but there is always someone behind us who provides what we need to make it through the day. There are different types of parachutes that we need either directly or indirectly, for support when our plane is shot down. Sometimes it's a physical parachute, a mental parachute, an emotional parachute, a spiritual parachute and sometimes even a financial parachute. Sometimes, in the daily challenges that life gives us, we miss what is important. We fail to say the simple but golden words like "hello," "please," or "thank you," acknowledge and congratulate someone, give a compliment, or just do something nice for absolutely no reason. Make sure that when you reach your heights you stay grounded and have gratitude for people who have been directly or indirectly responsible to help pack your parachute and help you reach where you are today. Remember that your success was not only because of you!

Emotion Management

VIII

"Stop letting people who do so little for you control your mind, feelings and emotions."

– Will Smith

The subject of managing emotions hangs around understanding your own emotions, expressing them appropriately and receiving other's emotions with caution.

The mind is an infinite space existing in a state of vacuum. It unconsciously picks up information around itself without any positive or negative discrimination. Interestingly, negative information, occupies more mind space despite lacking substance, just like a blown balloon. As a result, these negative thoughts get consciously played back at any point of time. This unavoidable phenomenon becomes the fundamental reason for all our agonies in life. Therefore, we are left with nothing but to manage ourselves in the presence of negativities. The solution is to dilute the existence of negativity by increasing our focus on positivity. If you wish to prove the small size of a pencil, place a bigger pencil beside it. This is a simple and practical approach which can be achieved by keeping ourselves engaged with good thoughts and activities and dilute the impact of negative thoughts. This is exactly what we do unconsciously in our daily life. During stress, frustration, anger, or depression, we try to run away from the situation and engage ourselves in activities which we enjoy doing. Unfortunately, some people select negative for negative e.g., smoking, drinking, junk food and other forms of addictions, which is not at all recommended. Others spend time in meditation, reading, watching motivational videos, art, craft, music, dance, movies, playing with children, or talking to family, and close friends etc. These activities help to divert our thoughts, relax, and makes us feel happy for that moment. Imagine if we routinely keep ourselves engaged in at least one of these activities irrespective of stress, tension, frustration, anxiety, or depression. Such structured engagements prepare us to manage emotional fluctuations through rationalization and prioritization. On a long run, our engagement become so profuse that we build ourselves into an emotionally stable person. People who seriously nurture their hobbies like dancing, singing, drama, writing, reading literature etc., are relatively immune to negativities in life.

Our emotions are not just restricted to us. Expression of emotions has a cascading effect on others. When you throw a stone into the water, you can watch the ripples created by the stone and they remain for quite some time even after the stone has settled down. Consider yourself as that stone. You may create splashes and settle down, but the waves generated will disturb the peace of all your fellow beings. This impact becomes even more significant if you hold a responsible position in your society or organization. The outburst of anger, frustration, disrespect, or jealousy will impact others. The same goes with expression of joy and happiness and you are responsible for both. We cannot contribute to world peace if we are riddled with inner conflict, hatred, doubt, or anger. We radiate the feelings and thoughts that we hold inside. Whatever is splashing inside us is spilling out into the world, either creating beauty or discord with other circles of life. Once I was speaking to my subordinate late in the evening over the phone. Suddenly, I heard his wife's shouting, and it was quite evident that she was either annoyed or disturbed. My subordinate was embarrassed once he realized that I heard his wife. He apologized for the disturbance. I took some courage to ask if everything was fine at his end. With some hesitation, he informed that this was the outcome of our morning meeting where the super boss was furious on him for a project delay. He had an explanation, but the boss was in no mood to accept any excuses. He was so disturbed with the incident that he missed to take his daughter to the park in the evening. As the daughter was accustomed to play in the park at that time, she started crying. Moreover, he also broke his promise to accompany his wife for shopping and thus the entire evening was messed up. This was a burning example to gauge the impact and extent of emotional outbursts in the corporate life on family and social life. Many a times seniors lose control over their emotions and vent out their dissatisfaction, for whatsoever reason, in an inappropriate manner and go away. But its repercussions on the subordinates continue for long and unfortunately the boss remains ignorant about everything. I took some efforts to council my subordinate. I am sure we do not want to experience such incidences in our life and, therefore, we should take care that we do not become the reason for someone's agony.

Once TT Rangarajan, a well-known motivational speaker said, "Everything that comes out of human body stinks. The sweat, the saliva, the blood, the urine, the stool, everything stinks. The only one thing coming out of the human body which we can avoid stinking are our words." Literature plays a vital role is expression of emotions. Interestingly, we can use good vocabulary not only to share good feelings but also to express unhappy emotions. For e.g. "How can you be so irresponsible?" can be better articulated as "Can you please explain why you missed to deliver your responsibility?" "I think you lack team handling capability" can be better articulated as "I think there is still some scope left to improve your team handling capacity." "Are you trying to bypass my authority" can be "In future I would like you to keep me informed about everything." Proper use of language helps you avoid use of derogatory, insulting, rude, demeaning, and racist words. People who use words carefully and honestly hardly have enemies. Personality is not because of looks but speech which reflects the state of mind of the person. So, if you wish to portray a respectable self-image you better check and weigh your words while speaking. Some people are of the opinion that the only way to get work done is through creating an atmosphere of fear by using loud, derogatory, and demeaning statement for even the slightest insignificant mistake. Under such stressful atmosphere the team loses motivation to do anything beyond instruction. Such managers miserably fail to bring out their team's best potential as the brain functions to its maximum capacity only in a free atmosphere. The same applies to a family atmosphere where utmost care is required to express your dissatisfaction or concern to your children or spouse or parents. It may be easy for you to forget but may not be for the other as he or she may be more emotionally sensitive resulting in a sour relationship.

Expression of emotions is also controlled by a person's sense of self-esteem or self-importance generally called as "ego" which gets automatically installed when a person achieves a lot. It acts as an invisible curtain which restricts free flow of opinion and expressions during conversations. People with high self-esteem have inhibitions in sharing their emotions to mask their vulnerability in front of others. They are their own doctors and consultants and believe in managing everything on their own. They pretend to be self-sufficient and independent. These people are more prone to stress which later result into cardiac disorders. They speak less as they have a fear that their intelligence and respect may get compromised due to difference in opinion. They avoid confronting or entering a debate for the same reason. However, that does not mean that these people are bad, or we should not mingle with them. It is worth to get connected with them as they carry valuable information and wisdom. But they would never be the one to take the first step. Once I was on a US trip to meet my colleagues who were the technical experts of my client's project in India. The most important meeting was with the project leader, a very senior, experienced, and renowned personality but very difficult to approach. In general, he was a nice person to talk but was disliked by many in the organization due to his fixed mindset. I knew it was going to be tough for me as he would directly or indirectly influence the outcome of my visit. However, I had great respect for him for his immense contributions to pharmaceutical technology in his career of more than three decades. I was mentally prepared to face him, that too for the first time in person. I entered his cabin, greeted him, and opened the conversation with some general talks. I took the opportunity to congratulate him for his achievements and appreciate his scientific contribution to the society. He was humble enough to thank me. He narrated details of few important inventions and shared his experience around it and, believe me, hearing the inventor himself was music to my ears. I was listening to him and trying to grab as much knowledge as possible just like a good student. We went for coffee, and he offered to accompany me for lunch to his favourite countryside restaurant. He proactively scheduled a meeting the next day with his entire team to brief the project details. He was very candid to share that he was loving the conversation with me, and he would like to have virtual connects once a week after I return to India. Although no project discussion happened that day, but I was very happy to have won his confidence and establish a personal rapport with him. While reading this if you have started thinking to talk to someone valuable but having ego issues, then there is good news. The good news is in this process of thinking about building relationship with that person you have started shedding off your own ego!

Ships don't sink because of water around them. They sink because of the water that gets in them. Don't let what is happening around you get inside you and weigh you down. I lost my father at a time when the pandemic was at its worst phase with very high death rate across the country. The situation was so bad that all direct flights were cancelled, and the connecting flights were taking more than a day to reach Kolkata from Mumbai. My mother acted very strong and asked me not to travel for the last rites as it would be a health risk for many, including me. My younger brother was already there to take care of the rituals, so I should not worry. It was an extremely tough call, but I decided to obey her considering the safety of my family. However, as the news spread, relatives and few close friends called to convey their sincere condolence. When they came to know that I would not be there as an elder son to carry out the rituals, they advised me to travel or else I would repent later. I lost strength and became a victim of emotions. I was sandwiched between practicality and tradition. On one hand I was feeling guilty and on the other hand I wanted to stay safe for my family. I am blessed to have a very strong mother who was firm with her decision and saved me to take such a big risk. Through this incidence, I learnt that it is important to hold on to your decisions irrespective of what people think or advise. People may be honest while advising, but they have no clue about the complexity of your problem. The issue magnifies for those with fame and popularity. People vent out their anger or dissatisfaction using abusive language in public even for personal matters. Some get so much impacted that they end up with psychological disorders. Protecting yourself from other's thoughts is self-care. You will never reach your destination if you stop and throw stones at every dog that barks. The less I care about other's opinion, the more I am free to be "Me." Happy people are the ones who hear everyone but walk the path like a lion on their own terms with no obligation to prove anyone.

Decision Management

IX

"Sometimes you make the right decisions, sometimes you make the decisions right."

Philip C McGraw

Our life is like a pearl necklace where each pearl represents a decision that we have taken during the journey. The beauty of the necklace depends on the quality and outcome of these decisions. Whenever you see success, it is an indication that someone once made a courageous decision and lived by it. Our present is because of our past decisions. It takes courage to take decision and stick to it. However, it is not as easy as it looks like. In general, we hesitate to take decisions due to the struggle between the right and the wrong and a fear of making mistakes in the process. The fear is usually related to lack of self-confidence. In fact, the fear to fail is already a prior indication of failure. Therefore, it is important to overcome the fear and sense of ambiguity between right and wrong in the process of decision making. If the decision can address your wellbeing and of the people around us, it should be sufficient for us to go ahead. There is nothing called as wrong decision. Either it is a right decision or an experience where we learn what we should not do. There will always be instances where we would feel or made to realize that we have landed up in a wrong decision for some reason or the other. In such a case, there is no point in going back and starting from scratch. In fact, it is an opportunity to stick to our decision and find legitimate ways to make it right. The quicker we learn to take decisions for ourselves and own them, the better the life becomes.

A couple with a decent family background were at the initial stage of their career. They had high ambitions but unfortunately their qualification was not sufficient to make it big in the country. After exploring all possible options, they decided to use their savings to move oversees for a better future. The wife got admitted in a pharmacy course and the husband decided to accompany her on a dependent visa. While the wife was studying the husband was going through severe challenges to make a living. He had to work at gas stations and grocery stores to earn money to meet the daily expenses. They stayed in shared apartments to avoid heavy expenses. They hardly had time to relax and spend time with each other. Their families were extremely worried and requested them several times to come back as they had sufficient money to manage a stress-free life in India. However, the couple was adamant on their decision. The husband learnt driving and got a driving license. He drove taxi for more than 12 hours a day for couple of years and made decent money. Meanwhile the wife also completed her course and added to the earnings by working in a hospital pharmacy. They sacrificed their weekends to generate double hourly income. Today they own a taxi, a car, and a home of their own in a foreign land with multiple properties in India.

They have not only helped themselves but are now able to help others as well. It was not their qualification but their courage to take a decision and own it which created an inspiring story.

Many families have a tradition of the eldest taking a decision for every event or occasion, irrespective of his or her knowledge of the matter. Typically, in a male dominated society, either the husband in a nuclear family or the eldest male member in a joint family is the decision maker. The others unconditionally obey despite their own reservations. In an Indian context, usually the wife becomes so used to her husband's decisions that after some time she losses her ability and confidence to decide. Matters like education, career and marriage of children are all driven by one person. The same applies to income, expenses, and investments. Many a times, the wife has no clue about her husband's income and financial planning. One of my friends met an unfortunate demise at a very early age. His wife was struggling with grief, but her bigger concern was managing the family finances as she was never exposed to any of these in the past. This is a major challenge in the society where many of us are not prepared for any unfortunate incidence. Some people take decisions not because they want to dictate but because the other does not want to get involved just for convenience. You will often come across a wife saying for her husband, "He is there, and he is wise enough to decide for his family, I am fine with whatever he decides." In this process, one person becomes overburdened with responsibilities which on a long run may impact his health. Therefore, it is fine to have someone to take a final call but only after involvement of the family members in the decision-making process. Let us not ignore children. It is our responsibility as parents to prepare them to take their own decision. Otherwise, they will always be used to parents deciding for them. The sooner they start taking their own responsibility, the quicker they would be prepared to face the challenges of the world. It is not what you leave for them that makes them great but what you leave in them, and decision-making ability is one of them. It all starts at home with baby steps!

During B. Pharma, my classmate and roommate was a very decent guy from Srinagar. Although he was inclined towards commerce, he accepted pharmacy as his father convinced him about the prospects of the course based on his friends' advice. For the 1st year, he was regular at classes and sincere with his assignments. We had become very good friends and without any hesitation, he used to reach out to me for clarifications. While explaining, I used to observe his struggle to understand the subjects. I was too young to understand the hidden problem and thought that he would somehow manage to sail through like few other students in the class. Unfortunately, despite his persistent efforts, he did not clear a single subject, not even the supplementary exams. I saw him very disturbed and irritated. He started missing classes and instead going to the mosque for seeking peace of mind. He argued with me whenever I tried to help him realize that he is deviating from the path. One morning I received his father's call on the landline as my friend was away from home. His father sounded extremely concerned for whatever is happening with his son. We discussed a lot about his challenges and possibilities to improve his situation. The same evening his father called him.

Immediately after the call, he took the train and left for Srinagar without any reservation, leaving behind all his belongings. I waited for him but could never get my best friend back. Decisions made for others without their consent can have a severe implication and should be avoided at any cost.

Once a very active lady aged 50 died due to an ailment. In addition to managing the household chores she used to oversee everything including child's education, care for the aged in-laws, engaging relatives, etc. She would express at times, "my house needs my time, my hubby can't even make a cup of coffee, my family needs me for everything, but no one cares or appreciates the efforts that I put in. I feel they all take me for granted". Within a span of three month of her death her husband had started playing tennis for an hour at his club. He took a inter departmental transfer to avoid travel anymore. He appointed a cook with a higher salary so that she would buy the groceries and provisions as well. He had appointed a fulltime caretaker for his aging parents. Kids started taking their own responsibilities and were also doing fine. Overall, life had started to return to normalcy. Remember that the lady had missed the school reunion for a minor ailment of her mother-in-law. She even missed her cousin's wedding because she had to supervise the repair work in her house. She sacrificed enjoying in so many parties and movies because her children had exams. But immediately after her death, two more maids were hired, and with just few adjustments the house was in order. Therefore, it is important to recover from the mindset that I am indispensable and without me the house will suffer. Your time is your time and there is no one to decide for you unless you do it yourself. Make time for yourself and your friends. Talk, laugh, and enjoy. Live your passion, live your life. Occasionally do things that you love to do. While there is nothing wrong to think about happiness for others, but it is wrong to search your happiness in others. You too deserve some happiness because if you are not happy you cannot make others happy. Everyone needs you, and you too need your own care and love. Although this example is about a housewife, but this also holds true for men who sacrifice their life to bring prosperity to their family. Let us take a strong decision to help ourselves and make this life worth living. Let us not risk our life as we all have only one life to live.

Deep in thoughts, every second person on the planet thinks about exploring the journey of entrepreneurship to achieve his or her dreams. In most cases, these thoughts are hardly converted to an executable decision as people have a fear of losing their comfort zone. But the truth is, when it feels scary to jump, this is exactly when you should jump. Otherwise, you end up staying in the same place for your entire life, unless you are desperate to achieve your dreams at any cost. The bigger risk is when people try to jump with a thought of trying and testing the journey. The thought is, "If I am successful its fine or else, I will go back to my job." This mindset is extremely dangerous when you play on the entrepreneurial ground. You cannot have a thought of a backup as this journey demands maximum acceleration with full throttle without looking back. A backup option will never let you leave your comfort zone and will always tend to find shelter of the sweet spot when you face challenges. The concept of Plan B does not hold good for entrepreneurial journey. People quit job but since they carry a contingency plan in their mind, they miss to give their 100%. This is one among the big reasons that most startups fail with extremely low success rate, even below 1%. Finally, they end up ruining their career in the process. The corporate reality is that once you quit, it is difficult to justify the gap in career and get back into job. Entrepreneurial journey is a one-way track. An entrepreneurial journey can only be successful when you decide unconditionally not to give up. You own your journey and decide to make it happen. You cannot sail across by dabbling your feet into the water. You must jump and learn to swim across.

The objective of every person at a very basic level is to move from point “A” to point “B.” We try not to leave any stone un-turned to make sure we keep growing in life. However, one fundamental fact which probably we do not realize in our journey from “A” to “B” is that if we want to move from “A” to “B” we have to leave “A.” We tend to move towards “B” with one foot still stuck at “A.” We keep ourselves so entangled with our past that it becomes almost impossible for us to take the leap of faith. Even if it is a tough decision, it is extremely important that we detach from the past otherwise we will have to compromise on our growth rate.

It is said that the entire life of a person flashes in front of his eyes before death. Think of the situation how painful that moment would be if the memories are full of regrets. But thinking about it at that point of time makes no sense when you are in no position to reverse them. In this context, I would like to introduce you to the book "The top five regrets of the dying" written by Bronnie Ware who used to work as a nurse in an Australian hospital and took care of patients living at the last stage of their life. While talking to these patients she realized that every person had a regret in their life. The interesting thing was although the patients were not related to each other, but their regrets were similar. Among all these, she picked up the most common and relevant five regrets for her book. The first regret was "I wish I had the courage to live a life true to myself not the life others expected from me." 2nd was "I wish I hadn't worked so hard". 3rd was "I wish I'd the courage to express my feelings". 4th was "I wish I had stayed in touch with my friends", and 5th was "I wish I had let myself be happier". Are you able to connect any of these regrets with your journey or have you already started feeling the gap between what you want and what is happening in reality? If the answer is yes, it is time to start thinking. Have you heard a dying person wishing to buy a house or a car or jewellery? No, while dying the regrets are not about materialistic things but about those who were around us, but we never cared to value their presence. The reason for sharing these regrets is to help you realize that if you believe in something for yourself then do not ignore or push it for future. I understand that in this fast and demanding world it is difficult to avoid a regretful ending. But if you still have time left, then take a firm decision to care for at least few of them now so that the burden of regret would be minimal and dying would be easier. Value presence to avoid regret of absence.

Health Management

X

"I believe that the greatest gift that you can give your family and the world is a healthy you."

Joyce Meyer

I do not want to sound like another health or fitness expert while dealing with this topic. The information on health on the social media has become overwhelming. Everyone seems to be an expert recommending something or the other based on what they have experienced or what they must have heard or read. This leads to a serious confusion to figure out what to be followed and what to be ignored. Something what you follow today becomes obsolete the other day after you watch another video on YouTube which makes it difficult to stick to one plan or decision. Everything seems to be important. Let us understand that health is a very personalized topic and must be visualized from an individual's perspective. It is you who can decide what makes you feel comfortable and happy while maintaining a good physical and mental health. In the process of health management, various elements like social, geographical, occupational, behavioural, cognitive, and emotional factors, directly or indirectly impact our wellbeing. What may work for you may not be true for the others. Restricting diet may be essential to support a good health due to your sedentary lifestyle but not for someone who works at the manufacturing plant or the construction site. Similarly, the types of exercise which must have helped others may not work for you because of a different body structure or an ailment. My fitness trainer mentioned that the extent of executing the most preferred exercise, walking, should depend on your lifestyle. People who live a dynamic lifestyle should have limited walking and more cardio or else they may end up with knee ailments with age due to excessive stress on the joints.

Like career, it takes time, efforts, and commitment to build and maintain a fit body and mind. The challenge today is although everyone is concerned but people lack patience and continuity. We get motivated by celebrities and athletes and become impulsive to achieve it as soon as possible. Then we start excessive dieting and carry out heavy workouts without consultation. These steps are extremely detrimental to health as the body takes its own time to adjust and we need to give it time. Despite being monitored by qualified trainers, many celebrities expose themselves to excessive workouts resulting in extreme stress. Recently, we have heard some unfortunate cases of celebrities losing their life during or just after workouts. A few years ago, I went on a 10-day detox tour to a yoga centre. Since my objective was weight loss, I was prescribed a liquid diet for the period with lots of water, several natural treatments, yoga, and meditation. Being surrounded by so many people with similar objective, I was super excited to follow the weight loss regime. I sincerely followed my prescription and lost 6.5 kgs in those ten days! Before returning, I was prescribed a healthy diet along with regular exercises. I tried but somehow could not cope up with the routine due to frequent travels and regained weight within a few months. The next year I went to the same centre to repeat the schedule but within a couple of days it became unbearable for me to withstand the crash dieting. I started craving for food which resulted in severe gastric issues. I had to give up within a few days and come back home. This may not happen with everyone, but after this experience I decided not to do anything extreme like this anymore. Rather, I have leveraged on technology and subscribed to a fitness app which has provided me a flexible online platform to balance my diet regime and workout schedule under supervision without disturbing my routine activities. My trainer never advocates aggressive dieting to avoid body being deprived of essential nutrients. She encourages to maintain a healthy and active lifestyle with intermediate workouts, walking, swimming, cycling, playing etc., whenever possible to whatever extent my body can withstand. I have not lost weight significantly but did not gain as well. By following the schedule regularly, I could overcome lethargy, body cramps and chronic health issues related to gastrointestinal disorders. I am keeping a good health and energy which helps me carry out multiple activities together without getting exhausted.

One of my friends, a music teacher, got an opportunity to join an online academy as a teacher. While she was very happy with her classes, she continuously complained of severe headache after every class. She has been a teacher for many years and such a problem was a bit unusual for her. She was worried that if this issue persists for long, she may have to compromise with her career. One evening, while having tea at our house, we generally discussed the sudden increase in internet use, that too with a high speed to enable seamless video calls. Out of curiosity, I asked her that she must be requiring a very high internet speed to support her online music classes. She agreed and that is when I connected it to her complains of headache. I casually advised her to switch off the internet at night before sleep. She started doing it and then never complained anymore. Today we are living in a web of radiations which has resulted in severe health challenges. Unfortunately, we cannot ignore this essential component of our lives, but at least manage to keep away from it as and when possible. Switching off Wi-Fi in the night reduces the radiations significantly and helps in sound sleep. It is also advised to avoid use of phone at least two hours before sleep. Sometimes, violence and aggressive debate that we watch on television can be extremely detrimental, especially for children, which gets embedded in their subconscious memory. Therefore, be careful in selecting what you see and what you allow your children to watch.

One of the reasons why health issues were not so severe in the past is because our ancestors were connected to nature. Presently, we are destroying the natural habitat to create concrete jungles where we hardly have access to the basic elements of life like soil and sunlight. Vitamin and mineral deficiency have become common. There are hardly prescriptions where these supplements are not prescribed. Our children are even more compromised as they prefer to stay home with their gadgets and have lost the enthusiasm and charm of playing in the field. It is important to fill this nutritional gap right from the beginning. Oil message, daily exposure to sunlight and breast feeding should be mandatory for infants at least till the age of two years to help them develop a good immune system. Children should be encouraged to go out to play outside with friends at least once in a day. Junk food, smoking, alcohol should be avoided, and seasonal fruits and vegetables should be added as an essential element of the diet. Walking in the morning should be preferred for exposure to sunlight. We should use our vacations to expose ourselves to the elements of nature. Rather than visiting another city, we should choose places with more greenery. Stays in village resorts should be preferred to get more access to the nature. Ayurvedic treatments should be preferred for chronic ailments and herbal wellness for body detoxification. A little additional expense to take care of a healthy lifestyle on a regular basis can reduce the probability of bankruptcy in case of a major ailment in the future. In ICU, it is not only about the pain of the unconscious patient. It is more about the agony of those helpless family members and friends who are sincerely praying and eagerly waiting outside to take the patient back home. If you care for your loved ones, then prepare yourselves to die because of age but not of ill health. In addition, do not forget to insure your health.

Health issues are bound to happen. It is also true that some illness takes their own time to cure. No one has ever lived a disease-free life. Therefore, the challenge is not the health but the manner we react to it. In most health-related cases, we panic or take decisions out of emotions. This increases the possibility to get exposed to some unethical healthcare practices. People start taking financial advantage of our concern. Several such instances were observed during the pandemic where a virtual crisis of some essential medicines and hospital beds were created for which patients had to bear exponential price. This malpractice continued for long till the authorities intervened. These all complicate the illness which otherwise could have been easily cured with time and adequate care, even at home. Few years ago, I had unbearable pain around the stomach. Upon consultation in a big hospital, the doctor prescribed an MRI scan which confirmed a stone of around 3 mm stuck at the ureter. The doctor requested my consent for laser surgery requiring an overnight hospitalization. Due to the pain, I had almost lost my thinking ability and was in no position to analyse the recommendation. I requested the doctor to do whatever it takes to help me get rid of the pain. He asked if I had a company insurance and balance available in it. Once I confirmed and consented, I was immediately shifted to the best room and prepared for the surgery scheduled the next morning. The ureter walls were inflamed during the laser surgery, so a stent was inserted to avoid painful urination and delayed recovery. Post-surgery, I had a tough time to manage the burning sensation during urination. After 15 days I had to revisit the doctor to remove the stent. This required another night of hospitalization to claim insurance. Although, I did not have to pay the bill, but I felt it was extraordinarily high. After complete recovery, my wife disclosed that the size of the stone was quite small which could easily be removed in a few days by hydrotherapy and the surgery of any kind could be avoided. I should have confirmed the root cause of the pain, got a temporary pain relaxation and gone for a 2nd opinion before taking decision to operate. My colleague who was responsible to deal with the insurance company also supported my wife's opinion and confirmed my concern related to high treatment cost. I realized that the doctor took advantage of my panic state of mind. This is more critical in cases of children where parents get nervous very soon and expose them to medicines even for minor ailments which otherwise could have been treated with grandmother's recipe.

The human body is always at work, if not physically, mentally it is always occupied. The intensity of involvement increases with age as we keep accumulating responsibilities, experiences, and memories. That is the reason why a child's mind is relatively free. Various emotions like fear, concern, anger, love, passion etc., haunt us even during sleep resulting in sleepless nights. Physically we may be sleeping, but mentally we are still alert. That is why many of us feel tired even after having 8 to 9 hours of sleep and get exhausted even doing nothing physically. While tiredness of the body is felt through pain in different parts of the body, the mind manifests its pain in the form of frustration, boredom, anger, uneasiness, restlessness, confusion etc. Like the body, the mind requires equal attention for relaxation and rest. Meditation is one of the best ways to relax the mind and the body together and bring them to harmony. Spending even around 15 to 30 mins for meditation once every day can keep you physically and intellectually alert for the rest of the day. The process of meditation guides you to a state of emptiness which keeps you away from world's three major affairs responsible to keep you occupied. First it keeps you in the state of having absolutely no desire for a little while, as even the smallest desire to have something may not allow you to relax. Second, it keeps you in the state of doing absolutely nothing. You are neither eager to learn nor know anything for a while. Third, it helps you forget who you are. You may have many labels and laurels that you or the world has conferred on you but for a while you are just a person breathing in flesh and bone. Relaxing the mind can help to increase its strength and efficiency. Remember that the body can withstand anything, it is the mind that you must convince.

Cognitive and social health play an important role in a person's overall well-being. A person who possesses a friendly nature and attends social gatherings is socially healthy. People who maintain a good relationship with family and friends through effective communication are healthier and happier than the isolated ones. Therefore, the concept of laughter therapy has become important in health clubs. A laughing person may not always be a happy person but laughing may help to induce happiness in his life. Let us start inculcating discipline and good habits in our daily life. The most interesting thing about them is that they do not cost money. Remember that the absence of good habits could be as destructive as a bad habit. A healthy body is a sign of a healthy mind, while unhealthy body weakens one's ability to succeed and excel in life.

Conclusion

One day, a small gap appeared in the cocoon, and a man who happened to pass by stood for long hours and watched how a butterfly was trying to get out through this small gap. A lot of time passed, the butterfly seemed to have abandoned its efforts, and the gap remained just as small. It seemed that the butterfly did everything she could, and that she had no more strength for anything else. Then the man decided to help the butterfly, he took a penknife and cut the cocoon. Butterfly came out immediately. But her body was weak and feeble, her wings were transparent, and they barely moved. The man continued to watch, thinking that the wings of the butterfly were about to spread and get stronger, and it would fly away. Nothing happened! For the rest of its life, the butterfly dragged along the ground with its weak body and un-spread wings. She was never able to fly, because of the person, wanting to help her. He did not understand that the effort to get out through the narrow gap of the cocoon is essential for the butterfly, so that the fluid from the body can pass into the wings and enable the butterfly to fly.

Life forces a butterfly to leave its shell with difficulty so that it could grow and develop. Sometimes it is effort that we need in life. If we were allowed to live without encountering difficulties, we would be deprived. We could not be as strong as we are now. We could never fly. It is okay to be guided or navigated by people around us but not handheld. This is our life, and we need to take its ownership independently all throughout its journey. Let us accept this fact to manage our life better.

It is a human tendency to have everything perfect. However, an ideal situation is seldom achieved due to differences in perception of perfection among individuals. Sometimes we even fail to meet our own expectation. Therefore, it would be an effort in vain to achieve perfection to satisfy either others or us. Moreover, there is always a gap of around 20% to achieve 100% perfection and this 20% gap demands 80% of our efforts, involvement, and attention. Considering limited time and energy available at our disposal, it is important to decide how we would like to spend our time. Life is a puzzle which is complete only when all the pieces are connected perfectly. Therefore, a holistic approach is required to manage all aspects together but without any obsessive desire of perfectionism. The beauty of life is in its imperfections. Do not try to get rid of them but deal with them sensitively.

You may be wondering why I missed a very crucial topic of managing time and children. The entire process of life management consumes time. If your intent is good and management process is productive, you need not worry about time. You just need to ensure that the time is not wasted in unproductive activities like gossiping, watching television and stuff like that.

The reason why I deliberately avoided the topic related to our children is because I realized that our children are always watching us. If I focus on managing myself, most of the job to manage them is already done. Therefore, it is an integral responsibility of each one of us to keep an eye on ourselves. If you wish to gauge the extent of your success in managing life, observe your children. Their success would be an indirect measurement of yours.

Rather than focussing on what could not be done, start focusing on what all are the possibilities. A man asked an artist, “How do you make such beautiful things from stone?” He replied, “Beauty is already hidden there, I just removed the extra stone.” Your happiness is hidden within you. Just remove your worries and discover a new world for yourself. We are all in the process of searching solution, but the secret is that the solution already lies within us.

Subhashis Chakraborty

www.ingramcontent.com/pod-product-compliance
Lightning Source LLC
La Vergne TN
LVHW041109150826
845673LV00007B/1977

9798891864979